iDentities

PAUL SELIGSON and DAMIAN WILLIAMS

WORKBOOK 2

Contents

Unit 1 .... Page 3

Unit 2 .... Page 8

Unit 3 .... Page 13

Unit 4 .... Page 18

Unit 5 .... Page 23

Unit 6 .... Page 28

Unit 7 .... Page 33

Unit 8 .... Page 38

Unit 9 .... Page 43

Unit 10 .... Page 48

Unit 11 .... Page 53

Unit 12 .... Page 58

Selected audio scripts .... Page 63

Answer key .... Page 67

1.1 What are your earliest memories of school?

A ▶1 Listen to Chris telling his friend Janet about his first day at college. Number pictures a–e in the correct order.

B ▶1 Listen again. True (T) or false (F)?
1 Chris went to bed very late the night before his first class.
2 He arrived late for class because he stopped for coffee on the way.
3 The lecturer saw him fall asleep.
4 Chris doesn't think he was as embarrassed as the lecturer.
5 He apologized and asked to talk to her at the end of class.

C Circle the correct options.

I used to work in an office. I enjoyed it at first, having my own desk and talking to customers on the phone, but after a few years, the novelty ¹*wore off / rushed off*. It wasn't the most interesting job to be honest, and my career never really ²*pulled off / took off*, so I decided to leave and go back to college. But on my last day, I thought I'd have some fun, and managed to ³*go off / pull off* a trick on one of my coworkers. He was quite lazy, and every day after lunch he used to shut himself in his office and ⁴*doze off / wear off* for a while. He thought nobody knew what he was doing, but we all did, and thought it was quite funny. So on my last day, he went into his office as usual, and I stood outside his office and called him. I knew he would just listen to the message on the answering machine on his desk and only pick up if he wanted to. I heard his phone ⁵*ring / rush off* and then go to the answering machine. I said, "David, this is the area manager, and I'm five minutes away from the office. I'm coming in to do an inspection." Well at that, he jumped up, opened the door and ⁶*wore off / rushed off* towards the exit, shouting, "If anyone comes, say I'm sick!" We all had a good laugh about that.

D Make it personal Complete the sentences so they're true for you.
1 My enthusiasm for _____ wore off when _____.
2 I have a vague recollection of _____.
3 I can still see _____ as if it were yesterday.

1.2 What innovative businesses do you know?

A Complete the conversations with the correct form of these verbs. There are two extra.

| allow | be | have | say | seem | taste | try |

1. A: Have you heard Jack's latest business idea?
   B: No, and I don't want to. Having good ideas _____ one thing, but he never acts on them.
2. A: Have you been to the new vegetarian diner on 16th Avenue?
   B: Yes! Some of their burgers _____ amazing!
3. A: How's the new business going, Sarah?
   B: Terrible. I hired a new assistant and everyone _____ complained about him.
4. A: Is this price correct?
   B: Yes sir, why do you ask?
   A: It's just that two hundred dollars _____ like a lot to me.
5. A: What are the results of the latest research, Diane?
   B: Well, more and more of our customers _____ they'd like us to improve our support service.

B ▶2 Circle the correct forms. Listen to check.

Statistics ¹*vary / varies*, but it is generally believed that almost all new start-ups ²*fail / fails*. Some people say the figure is as high as 90 percent, which ³*seem / seems* high, but it's a reality. Everyone ⁴*have / has* at least one great idea, but building a successful company ⁵*take / takes* a lot of work and courage. Knowing a few basic facts first ⁶*help / helps*. For example, is the market already crowded? Several hours using search engines ⁷*is / are* a good place to start. Many start-ups also ⁸*has / have* hidden costs that often no one ⁹*discover / discovers* until it's too late. In general, people ¹⁰*make / makes* mistakes with start-ups. Make sure it's not you!

C Complete the sentences with an appropriate form of the verbs in parentheses.

1. The company, as well as its customers, _____ at all happy with its level of service. (be)
2. Everyone in the meeting _____ the new product will be a success. (think)
3. One of the managers _____ the new logo. He said it was too old-fashioned looking. (like)
4. Two years _____ a long time to develop a new product. It usually takes about 12 months. (be)
5. About a third of new businesses _____ successful this year. That's a great result. (be)

D Make it personal Complete the sentences so they're true for you.

1. Everyone in my class _____.
2. Both my parents _____.
3. These days, a lot of people _____.

How many ways can you use a brick? 1.3

A Read the first paragraph. Is the article going to contain good advice?

The art of procrastination

Do you have what it takes to be a good procrastinator? Or do you worry that you don't spend enough time worrying about not working on that important project? Well, now you don't have to worry, with this helpful guide. Read on to find out how you, too, can join the millions of other successful procrastinators out there, and avoid staying on top of things.

1 _____

Before you start work, make sure everything is in place. You need the right amount of space, the correct temperature, and enough time. You shouldn't be too hungry or too full, and you need to be able to tune out any unnecessary distractions. Don't even think about starting work until these conditions are met. Otherwise, you won't be able to produce the best work you can do. And only the very best is good enough.

2 _____

You have to answer every email as soon as it comes in. No one likes being ignored, and people hate it when you don't reply for a long time. Besides that, you might miss out on some fantastic deals and offers from that company you once bought a specific type of coffee from online. How could you, after they went to all the trouble of sending it to you? Only you.

3 _____

Changing your environment might just let your mind wander. It might even stimulate your brain, and you don't want that winning idea to just hit you like that. You need to zero in on exactly what you're doing!

4 _____

There's no way you can do any meaningful work if you don't keep abreast of current affairs. This means, obviously, trawling as many news sites as you can, as well as cross-checking facts between sites. You don't want to be ignorant!

5 _____

And I mean everything. When you're about a third of the way into a task (shame on you for getting so far), stop and ask yourself, "Is this really any good? I'm sure I could do better." If an idea pops into your head about how to do something differently, follow up on it. The best way forward at this point is usually just to tear it up and start from scratch.

Finally, the most important thing: if it's too difficult, just leave it. Never do today what you can put off until tomorrow.

B Read the rest. Put the headings back into the article 1–5. Then circle the best advice.

| Keep up with the world.   Don't be rude.   It has to be perfect. |
| Question everything.   Always work in the same place. |

C Complete the sentences with one missing word.
1 If you have trouble thinking of ideas, it can be good to just let your mind ^ for a while. *wander*
2 It's really hard to work with all that noise going on, I keep tuning.
3 That's when it hit: I could give my presentation as a story.
4 Some people listen to music while they work, but I need silence to really zero on what I'm doing.
5 Sally's best ideas usually pop her head when she's on the bus to work.
6 You need to prioritize these tasks if you're going to stay on of things.

1.4 What do the 2000s make you think of?

A ▶3 Complete the interview with the correct form of the verbs in parentheses. Listen to check.

PRESENTER: Hello and welcome to *Movie Watch*. Joining me today is movie director Jermaine Gómez. Jermaine, in your opinion, what ¹_____ (be) the most important movies of the decade so far?

JERMAINE: Well for me, one of the best films I ²_____ (see) in the last few years is *Her*, which came out in 2014. Until then, nobody ³_____ (make) a movie that was such an honest portrayal of impossible romance. I mean, yes, directors ⁴_____ (try) to do something similar with movies for years, but it had exactly the right combination of script, music, and acting that made it such a success.

PRESENTER: I agree, it's a great movie. Are there any others?

JERMAINE: Have you seen *Boyhood*? Critics ⁵_____ (describe) it in glowing terms, and they're not wrong. The makers of this movie did something no one ⁶_____ (ever do) before. They filmed it over 12 years, with the same actor as he aged from 6 to 18.

PRESENTER: I ⁷_____ (not watch) it yet, actually, but I'm definitely going to!

JERMAINE: Perhaps the best movie of the decade, though, is *Inception*, in my opinion. With this movie, they ⁸_____ (create) an insanely complicated story, which is thrilling to watch from start to finish, and great fun to try to figure out!

B Circle the correct options.

What ¹*has / had* been the most important technological innovation of the twenty-first century so far?

Many people would argue that it was the iPod. Until it came out, people ²*have / had* bought music on CDs, and some had huge collections that took up vast amounts of space in their home. Others might say the invention of social networking ³*has had / has been having* the most influence on our lives, but it ⁴*hasn't helped / didn't help* our privacy, as we now share pretty much everything online with the rest of the world. For me though, one of the biggest milestones was when IBM's computer "Watson" competed on the U.S. quiz show *Jeopardy*, and won against the two all-time champions. It was important because

it showed just how far we ⁵*have come / have been coming* in developing artificial intelligence. Until this point, many companies ⁶*had / have* been trying to develop computers capable of independent thought, and since then, this field ⁷*has / had* been developing rapidly. So much so that you can even talk to your cell phone and have it search the Internet for you.

C Match 1–5 to a–e to make sentences.

1 Usain Bolt set
2 3D printing is yet to set
3 The latest album by *Robotix* is set
4 The government has recently set
5 Video-sharing websites have set

a ☐ for a March release.
b ☐ the stage for a new generation of entertainers.
c ☐ a new world record for the fastest 100 meters in 2008.
d ☐ the world on fire, but is expected to become more popular in the next few years.
e ☐ new rules for opening a small business.

Have you ever had a dream come true? 1.5

A Read the autobiographical narrative and circle the correct options.

A chance encounter

Five years ago, something happened to me that would change my life forever. I was working as a cook in a restaurant on the other side of town, and ¹*I'd just finished / I've just finished* a really long shift. It ²*snowed / had been snowing* all day, so the drive home was taking longer than usual. I ³*just stopped / had just stopped* at the intersection when I felt a hard bump – someone ⁴*was driving / had driven* their car into the back of mine. I was furious.

I got out of the car to speak to the driver, and then I ⁵*had seen / saw* her. She ⁶*was / had been* the most beautiful woman I had ever seen. I couldn't help but remain speechless as she apologized profusely. In that single moment, all that anger and fatigue just washed away. She explained that she ⁷*had been looking / has been looking* for her turn, and by the time she saw I had stopped, it was too late. We exchanged information, and then just started chatting. Before we knew it, an hour had passed and we were both getting cold, so we ⁸*went / had gone* our separate ways. But before we did, we arranged to meet again and go for dinner.

Anyway, we got along really well, and two years ago, we ⁹*have gotten / got* married. She's made me so happy, and she tells me she feels the same, all the time. ¹⁰*We've had / We'd had* a beautiful baby girl, and we now have another one on the way. And yes, we're both very careful drivers now!

B Replace the words in bold with one of these expressions with *but*.

| all but certain | couldn't help but | nothing but sheer | I did nothing but |

1 I couldn't believe I'd passed the exam. It was **100%** luck! _____
2 I was so tired the next day. **All I did was** sleep. _____
3 Cathy was **so sure** she would never meet the right person. _____
4 I **was accidentally able to** overhear what they were saying. _____

C Complete the conversations with one word in each blank.

1 **A:** Let's _____ it. We need to find out more about the neighborhood before we decide to move there.
   B: That's _____ sure. Let's do some more research.
2 **A:** How long have Judy and Kevin been together?
   B: You're _____ me? How would I _____?
3 **A:** Have you thought about giving sailing a try?
   B: I have, but I don't think I'd be very good at it. Maybe I should just try it and see.
   A: That's _____ I'm telling you. Just _____ it a try. You won't know until you do.

D Look back at lessons 1.1–1.5 in the Student's Book. Find the connection between the song lines and the content of each lesson.

E ▶4 Listen to the five question titles from the unit, and record your answers to them. If possible, compare recordings with a classmate.

2 » 2.1 What would you change about your lifestyle?

A ▶5 Listen to the first part of a conversation between Charlotte and Gavin. Answer the questions.

1. Is Gavin enjoying his job?
2. How does his boss react to Gavin's work?
3. What has Gavin been thinking about doing?
4. Does he have a Master's degree?

B ▶6 Listen to the second part. What opportunity does Gavin have? Does Charlotte think it's a good idea?

C ▶6 Listen to the second part again. Complete the sentences from the conversation.

1. I know it sounds a little _____ - _____ .
2. You can't just sit around and wait for something else to _____ into your _____ .
3. They just seem like really _____ _____ right now.
4. You'll go the _____ _____ and work better.
5. You can still _____ _____ your degree.
6. I know if you _____ your _____ to it, you can make things work.

D Rearrange the words in italics to complete the motivational memes. Circle the one you like best.

1. *mile / go / extra / the* – you'll be surprised at what you can achieve.
   _____

2. *try / expectations / to / people's / never / meet* – but try your best, and you might exceed them.
   _____

3. *if / mind / you / your / it / to / put*, you can accomplish great things.
   _____

4. Go out and find your dreams – *wait / your / into / them / don't / lap / fall / to / for*.
   _____

E Match 1–4 to a–e to make sentences. There's one extra.

1. I'm sorry, but I'm afraid your qualifications don't meet
2. Alex's explanation of why he was late
3. Chris and Angela are working towards
4. I don't think it's such an unattainable

a ☐ target to increase sales by 20% this year.
b ☐ a solution to the marketing problem right now.
c ☐ the requirements of the job.
d ☐ a lot at stake.
e ☐ was so far-fetched that no one believed him.

What's the biggest house you've ever been to? 2.2

A Complete the text with these words. There are two extra.

don't   doesn't   hasn't   have   isn't   to   won't

MY HOME, MY WAY

The TV show that follows people as they make big changes to the places where they live

This week on *My Home, My way*, the Meyer family is having problems. They've just bought an expensive new sofa and realize they shouldn't ¹_____ , as it's going to put them over their budget. They also discover that although they want to extend their kitchen on the side of their house, they may not be able ²_____ . They really like the idea, but it seems their neighbors ³_____ .

Meanwhile, on the other side of town, Joe and Lily can't seem to agree on anything. Lily is eager to create an office in their spare room, but Joe ⁴_____ . He's always wanted to have a game room, but she ⁵_____ .

B ▶7 Circle the correct options to complete the excerpts from the TV show. Listen to check.

1 **TV PRESENTER:** So, I hear you've decided on a sofa?
  MR. MEYER: Yes, I love this sofa, and Jenny does, *too / to*. We're really happy with it.
  MRS. MEYER: Yes, we *have / are*.
  TV PRESENTER: But did you realize it's put you over your budget?
  MRS. MEYER: Oh no, we *weren't / didn't*!
  MR. MEYER: Well, I guess we can dip into our savings, just a few dollars.
  MRS. MEYER: I don't like that idea. *They're / It's* all we've got!

2 **MRS. MEYER:** So, do you think the neighbors will complain about the kitchen?
  MR. MEYER: Yes, I think they *might / do*. They didn't seem very happy about it earlier.
  MRS. MEYER: Oh, but I've always wanted a big kitchen!
  MR. MEYER: I know, I *am / have*, too.

3 **JOE:** We need to put stairs in behind this room.
  LILY: Oh no, stairs *take / takes* up much too space.

4 **LILY:** So, this is our spare room, which we're going to convert into an office. We've always wanted *to / too*.
  JOE: Wait, what? No, we *haven't / didn't*! I thought we were going to have a game room, with a pool table. That's what I told you.
  LILY: No, you *weren't / didn't*!

C Replace the underlined phrases with one word.

1 I've always wanted a big house, but my husband <u>doesn't want a big house</u>. He thinks it'll take too long to clean! _____

2 I bought an apartment last year, but I shouldn't <u>have bought an apartment</u>. I really miss having a back yard. _____

3 I love this area, and my girlfriend <u>loves this area</u>, too. But it's just too expensive to buy anything here. _____

4 I've never lived away from my parents, and my best friend hasn't <u>lived away from her parents</u>. We can't wait to move in together. _____

5 I've never thought about buying my own place, but I <u>might buy my own place</u> soon. _____

D Make it personal Rewrite two sentences in C so they're true for you.

1 _____
2 _____

2.3 Do you like to spend time alone?

A Read the people's advice. Match each person to photos A–D.

How to survive being alone in social situations

Whether it's going to a party or having a meal, how do you survive being alone in social situations? We asked four people for their tips.

1 Brynn Frazier ☐ First things first, choose the best time to go. On Saturday evenings, you usually get a lot of couples, so if you go then, you'll most likely wind up feeling lonely. I find the best time to go is in the afternoon. It's less crowded then, so you'll be able to savor your solitude in a space of your own. Also, try to arrive just before the movie starts. That way it'll already be dark, and people won't see you sitting there all alone.

2 Jerome Wolfe ☐ I often end up doing this when I'm traveling for work, so I know what it's like. The main thing you'll find is that it can be quite tedious waiting for your dish to be brought out. So take a book, or some headphones to watch a movie on your phone. Reading or watching something while you eat means you'll take your time, too. Don't be tempted to people watch though – other people don't like being stared at while they eat!

3 Ella McCormick ☐ People think I'm crazy for going away on my own, or "traveling light," as I say. But I wouldn't have it any other way. I get to go exactly where I want and do exactly what I want, which my friends don't. Even if that means just lounging around by the pool each day! I get to do it guilt-free. I find I experience things much more clearly when I see them through my own eyes, without another person's perception of the experience. So my advice if you're in this situation is just relax and enjoy it!

4 Alison Taylor ☐ This can be one of the hardest situations to be alone in, I think, especially if you don't know many people there. If you only know one or two people there, don't be tempted to stick with them all night. Nobody likes a shadow, and you may end up alienating them from other guests. Most of all, don't worry about being shy. In fact, be open about it. Find another guest who is on his or her own and make a joke about it. I did this recently and we got along really well. It also made it easier to mingle with other people as we were together.

B Read the advice again and complete 1–5 with the correct name. There's one extra statement.

1 _____ thinks other people might spoil the experience.
2 _____ says you shouldn't take too many things with you.
3 _____ says you need to make the experience interesting.
4 _____ thinks you should be honest about how you're feeling.
5 _____ thinks it's best if people can't see you.

C Complete the sentences with these words. There's one extra.

| cater | convey | crave | peace and quiet | restaurants | sense of | tastes | ubiquitous | upscale |

1 Sometimes even very sociable people _____ a bit of _____ .
2 The idea of traveling alone can _____ a _____ freedom to some.
3 When you're in a large group, it can be difficult to _____ to everyone's individual _____ .
4 It's less common to see people dining alone in _____ _____ .

Are you more of a morning or an evening person? 2.4

A Complete the sentences with *so* or *such*.

1 There are _____ many distractions here. I need to go to the library to study.
2 This is _____ a useful app to help organize your time. I recommend you try it.
3 I find it _____ difficult to concentrate in the afternoon. It makes _____ a big difference if I work in the morning.
4 Try prioritizing what you have to do. It'll make things _____ much easier for you.
5 You've worked really hard on this. Thank you _____ much!
6 There are _____ few ways to get a healthy energy boost.

B Choose the correct option (a, b or c) to complete the text.

I've recently started doing something new, which has made ¹_____ big difference to how productive I am. Twice a week, I schedule "meetings with myself." I actually schedule the time in my calendar, and during that time, I don't answer emails (I get ²_____ coming in all the time), don't answer the phone, or do anything else. There are ³_____ ways of avoiding the distractions usually, but this makes it ⁴_____ easier. It's made ⁵_____ big difference, and I get through my work ⁶_____ faster now.

1	a so a	b such a	c such	4	a so much	b such a	c so many
2	a so	b so much	c so many	5	a so a	b such a	c such
3	a so many	b such little	c so few	6	a so much	b so	c so many

C 🔊8 Correct the mistake in each conversation. Listen to check.

1 **A:** What's wrong? You look a bit stressed.
  B: Oh, I've just got so much things to do, I don't know where to start.
  A: Can I do some of them for you?
  B: Thanks, that would help so much!

2 **A:** Kate tells me you've started working from home two days a week.
  B: Yes, it's made such big difference. I can work without so many distractions. It gets so busy in our office.

3 **A:** This new organizer app is great. The only thing is, it costs $30.
  B: What? Why does it cost so?
  A: It's not so expensive when you see what it can do. It's so useful. Let me show you.

4 **A:** How was your vacation?
  B: Great, thanks. I feel such better now.
  A: Yes, you look a lot better. You were working so much before you went away.

D Circle the correct option.

1 Sorry I didn't make much sense on the phone this morning. I'd just woken up and was still feeling *hectic / drowsy*.
2 Can I grab a cup of coffee before we start revising our report? I need a bit of an energy *drag / boost*.
3 I'm so glad the day's over. Time felt like it was really *dragging / hectic*.
4 Things have been really *drowsy / hectic* lately. I've been finding it hard to stay on top of my studies.
5 Kate's really nervous about the presentation. She said she didn't *sleep / drag* a wink last night.

E **Make it personal** Complete the sentences so they're true for you.

1 _____ has made such a big difference to my life.
2 I find learning English so _____.
3 I have so little _____.

2.5 Can an apartment be too small?

A Read Jerry's email to Doug. Does Jerry prefer one of the places or does he like them both?

Doug Owen (dowen@everymail.id)

Hi Doug!

How is everything? Really pleased to hear you're moving here to start college. It'll be great to see you more often. In your email, you ask about the two areas you're thinking about moving to.

Both Lakeside and Oak Grove are nice areas, but ¹_____ . Sandra much prefers Lakeside, but I don't. The lake is great in the summer. We usually hang out there on weekends and grill food outside. ²_____ , it's really peaceful. You won't be disturbed by noise or anything while you're doing your college work at home. ³_____ , for me it feels a bit too isolated. You'd definitely need a car, as there aren't many stores or amenities nearby. Houses are pretty expensive there, too.

Oak Grove, ⁴_____ , is really centrally located. You'd be living a stone's throw away from stores and everything else you might need. Moreover, the public transportation connections around there are so much better than Lakeside. Having said that, it's not as quiet or safe as Lakeside. ⁵_____ it's not particularly dangerous, there is more crime than in other parts of the city.

So what do you think? In my opinion, ⁶_____ good places to live. It just depends what sort of thing you want. Sandra and I are over in Queen's Park, which is near both of them. So you'll have no excuse not to come and visit!

All the best,

Jerry

B Complete 1–6 in the email with these phrases.

> although   each has its pros and cons   however   in addition
> on the other hand   the two areas are both

C Complete the second sentence so it has the same meaning as the first. Use the words in parentheses.
1 Both apartments have good things and bad things. (CONS)
   Each apartment _____.
2 The house is huge, and it has a swimming pool. (ADDITION)
   The house is huge. _____.
3 Our kitchen is modern, but our dining room is old-fashioned. (HAND)
   Our kitchen is modern. _____, is old-fashioned.
4 Oakdale and New City are cheap places to live. (BOTH)
   The two areas _____.

D Look back at lessons 2.1–2.5 in the Student's Book. Find the connection between the song lines and the content of each lesson.

E ▶9 Listen to the five question titles from the unit, and record your answers to them. If possible, compare recordings with a classmate.

3.1 What language would you least like to learn?

A ▶10 Listen to three people describing a learning experience. Match each one to photos 1–6.

1 Valeria ☐   Leon ☐   Julia ☐
2 Valeria ☐   Leon ☐   Julia ☐
3 Valeria ☐   Leon ☐   Julia ☐
4 Valeria ☐   Leon ☐   Julia ☐
5 Valeria ☐   Leon ☐   Julia ☐
6 Valeria ☐   Leon ☐   Julia ☐

B ▶10 Listen again and answer the questions.
Which person …
1 thinks people have the wrong impression of her? _____
2 gave up for a while and then started again? _____
3 was reluctant to start at first? _____
4 enjoys something which other people think isn't interesting? _____
5 hasn't made steady progress? _____
6 has entered a competition? _____

C ▶10 Complete the sentences with one word. Listen again to check, if necessary.
1 I couldn't even get a half-decent sound out of it, and felt really out of my _____ .
2 I put a lot of _____ into it, practicing every day.
3 Although I was a bit _____ at first, soon it all came back to me.
4 Then I started jogging, and, to my surprise, I just sort of _____ it up naturally.
5 Since then I've joined a club, and I've improved by _____ and bounds.
6 People see me as a sort of "techy" person, but I think that's _____ .
7 I always just sort of _____ by when I need to and hope for the best.

D Make it personal Choose three of the expressions in C and write true sentences for you.
1 _____
2 _____
3 _____

13

3.2 Are you into tweeting?

A Look at the **bold** words and expressions, but don't read the descriptions yet. Do you know what they mean? Do you use them?

Trolling ¹[is / means / What / to / this] post comments in order to deliberately get a reaction from people. Why it became used on the Internet ²[relates / think / we / to / back] a 17th-century use of the word, which was to use bait when fishing, e.g. use something false to capture the naïve (in this case the fish).

Meh ³[became / this / Why / popular / so] we're not really sure. This three-letter word shows that you're not really interested in something. ⁴[interesting / that / is / What's] it can be an adjective (It was all very "meh") and even a noun (I refer you back to my last "meh").

Cupertino This is the nightmare of autocorrect. ⁵[was / from / came / Where / it] an early spell-checker program which knew the word "Cupertino" (the town where Apple has its head office), but not the word "cooperation." ⁶[was / What / do / would / it] correct the word "cooperation" to "Cupertino" every time someone tried to use it.

I can't even! ⁷[expression / What / know / we / is / about / this] that it began when a social media user finished a comment with "I can't!" to show he or she was speechless with shock or surprise. When the "even" was added, ⁸[really / we / know / don't], but it's clear that it was added to make the phrase even stronger.

B Order the words in italics in the texts above to make information-focus clauses.

1 _____   5 _____
2 _____   6 _____
3 _____   7 _____
4 _____   8 _____

C Match 1–5 to a–e to make sentences. Decide if each sentence contains a subject clause (S) or an object clause (O).

1 How often people use this expression
2 Whether it's appropriate to send a direct message
3 When exactly we started using hashtags
4 Why social media became so popular
5 What we did to make messages shorter

a ☐ we're not really sure. _____
b ☐ was a result of many different factors. _____
c ☐ was to use lots of abbreviations. _____
d ☐ reflects how much they use social media. _____
e ☐ I think depends on how well you know the person. _____

D ▶ 11 Circle the correct option. Listen to check.

1 A: Do you think social media has made us more sociable?
   B: To a certain *respects / extent*, yes, as long as we remember to meet people face-to-face sometimes!
2 A: I don't get your post. It's confusing to say the *least / mildly*.
   B: Meh, don't worry about it. I can't be bothered to explain.
3 A: What do you use social media for?
   B: Mainly for keeping in touch with my family. It's like a virtual get-together, if you *speak / will*.
4 A: I love seeing all the new memes that come out after a big news event.
   B: Me too. In some *respects / extent*, it's like a more honest representation of modern culture.

E Make it personal Complete the sentences so they're true for you.

1 Why people use social media so much I _____.
2 When exactly I started using social media was _____.

14

Can someone learn to be a good speaker? 3.3

A Read and match the types of presenters below to 1–5.

| The Animator | The Entertainer | The Lecturer | The Motivator | The Storyteller |

The five most common types of speakers

1 _____

These types of presenters see themselves as coaches, someone who will motivate you to achieve your goals (often goals that you didn't realize you needed to have). They give lots of encouragement through buzzwords such as "You've got this" and "I believe in you," and you're likely to leave the presentation feeling like you can climb Mount Everest. Be careful though. It's easy to get caught up in all the hype and set yourself impossible goals. And this presenter will make you keep your word. He or she will want to see real outcomes, and if you make any promises, you won't be able to take back your words.

2 _____

This person loves the sound of his or her own voice, and will use every trick in the book to grab your attention, from jokes to film clips. He or she may have a great reputation as a speaker, spread by word of mouth. Sitting in this presentation will no doubt be a lot of fun, but you may come away wondering if you've actually learned anything useful.

3 _____

Naturally gifted, this presenter is a real joy to watch. From the get-go he or she will have you transfixed, using compelling personal anecdotes and imagery to guide you through the content of the presentation. It's as if the presenter were born to spread the word. Time will fly through this presentation and you won't want to leave at the end.

4 _____

This person is lost without slides. He or she will prepare for hours beforehand, gathering data and putting together slides which zoom in and out, with all the whistles and bells. It's entertaining up to a point, but often it'll get to be too much, and you might get motion sickness. If anything goes wrong with the technology, the presenter will come unstuck, tripping over words and generally crashing and burning.

5 _____

This presenter also loves the sound of his or her own voice, and not only that, often has an inflated sense of self-worth. The presenter loves to back up points with references to books and quotations to show that he or she knows much more than you. Your job is to listen, no matter how boring the style of delivery is. The presenter has to have the final word, so is unlikely to offer the opportunity to ask questions. If he or she does, you won't be able to get a word in edgewise during the answer.

B Re-read. True (T), false (F), or not enough information (NI)? Which type of speaker would you most like to be?

1 The Animator is good at coping with problems.
2 The Entertainer is usually a failed actor.
3 The Lecturer has read a lot of books.
4 The Motivator might make you do something you don't want to do.
5 The Storyteller is talented at keeping your attention.

C Match the highlighted expressions with *word* in the text to the meanings below.

1 tell as many people as possible _____
2 don't break a promise _____
3 through personal recommendations _____
4 change what you said before _____
5 say the last thing _____
6 have trouble saying _____
7 impossible to interrupt _____

3.4 What's the ideal age to learn a language?

A ▶12 Complete 1–6 with participle clauses, using the verbs in the box. There are two extra. Listen to check.

| arrive | encourage | feel | grow up | learn | meet | start | think |

The life of a polyglot

¹_____ in a family which traveled a lot, as a child Annika Simms came into contact with a wide range of different languages. ²_____ with English, she then went on to learn French, German, Russian, and Turkish. She now speaks more than 15 languages. ³_____ by her parents when she was a child, she would often make friends and "tune in" to the language they used. "⁴_____ in a new country," says Annika, "my parents would first teach me a few phrases. When ⁵_____ other kids, I would try these out, and then gradually pick up more and more of the language. It became easier and easier everywhere we went." ⁶_____ confident in her language abilities, Annika now works as an interpreter for the UN.

B Complete the second sentence so that it means the same as the first. Use a participle clause.

1 Before he became famous, Brad Pitt delivered refrigerators.
_____, Brad Pitt delivered refrigerators.

2 Jon Bon Jovi grew up in Pennsylvania and sold newspapers as a teenager.
_____, John Bon Jovi sold newspapers as a teenager.

3 As he was working as a support act, Jim Carrey made a lot of useful contacts in his early career.
_____, Jim Carrey made a lot of useful contacts in his early career.

4 Because he hoped to become a soccer player, Rod Stewart tried out for Brentford F.C in 1960.
_____, Rod Stewart tried out for Brentford F.C in 1960.

5 When she signed her first modeling contract, Cindy Crawford had had few jobs beforehand.
_____, Cindy Crawford had had few jobs beforehand.

C Correct one mistake in each comment 1–5. Check (✓) the tips you would find useful.

> **JANA PABLO:** What do you do to learn English? Any tips?
>
> 1 **FRANCISO GUERRA:** Having learn new vocabulary, I write it on little notes and stick them around my apartment, so I see them every day and remember the words.
> 2 **LEE WU:** Where sitting on the bus, I listen to podcasts in English.
> 3 **GABRIELLA VEGA:** After had read a text, I highlight all the new words and look them up.
> 4 **ANNA MACIAS:** Having hearing some new phrases, I try to use them the same day when speaking to people.
> 5 **BRUNO KAYA:** I take photos of signs I see in the city. After having taking them, I go home and look up any new words.

D Make it personal Add your own comment with a tip for C.

_____

What can't you learn through practice? 3.5

A Read the essay and choose the best title (a, b, or c).
a The best way to learn a new language.
b It's easy to learn another language.
c How I learned to stop worrying and speak another language.

I've heard a lot of different advice for learning a language, from studying grammar to practicing speaking with friends. But one thing remains constant: you need to be confident enough to give it a try. But what happens if you're not very confident in another language?

1 _____ I love languages, and I find studying them very interesting, but being a bit shy, even in my own language, I've found it difficult. Having made a lot of progress with this recently, however, I'd like to share two techniques that have really helped me.

2 _____ First, think of a situation that you always tend to avoid because you worry about how you will cope (e.g. on the telephone). Having chosen a situation, use whatever techniques you can to make yourself understood. And don't be afraid to ask people to repeat what they said, or speak more slowly. You'll often find that the second time you hear something, it sinks in. Over time, you'll start to become less afraid of these situations and your vocabulary – and confidence – will grow.

3 _____ A good way to do this is to imagine the worst thing that can happen when you do. People are generally nice and accommodating, and won't laugh at you. If they do, then they're not the kind of people you want to talk to anyway. In no time at all, you'll feel more comfortable making mistakes, and you'll become more fluent – and confident.

These are a couple of ways that have helped me. Nowadays I feel much more confident when speaking another language, and it shows!

B Complete the essay with topic sentences a–d. There's one extra.
a Put yourself in a situation where you have to speak the language.
b This has always been my problem.
c Try to avoid making mistakes.
d Remember that it's OK to make mistakes.

C Complete the extracts from another essay with these words.

| beginning | first | matter | time | then | while |

In the ¹_____ , I found making friends really difficult in another language. But after a ²_____ , my confidence grew and I was able to speak to people more. In no ³_____ at all, I was talking to people all the time. Even people waiting at the bus stop!

Having grown up in the same city all my life, I've never had much contact with people from other countries. ⁴_____ one day I decided to travel abroad for a short vacation. ⁵_____ , I found it really difficult and was very homesick, but in a ⁶_____ of weeks, I was enjoying it. I made lots of new friends and, over time, I came to love traveling. Having been to more than ten different countries now, I'm forever planning my next trip.

D Look back at lessons 3.1–3.5 in the Student's Book. Find the connection between the song lines and the content of each lesson.

E ◯ 13 Listen to the five question titles from the unit, and record your answers to them. If possible, compare recordings with a classmate.

17

4 » 4.1 How often do you remember your dreams?

A ▶14 Listen to Jaylan and Sue discussing an article about dreams. Check (✓) the things it says can influence your dreams.

1. ☐ what you eat before going to bed
2. ☐ good and bad smells
3. ☐ stress
4. ☐ your star sign
5. ☐ playing video games
6. ☐ being a creative person

B ▶14 Listen again and complete Jaylan's notes.

* German study: [1]_____ volunteers in two groups
* R.E.M. = the stage of your sleep when you [2]_____
* Lucid dreaming = the ability to take [3]_____ of your dreams
  Lucid dreamers can [4]_____ off nightmares
* Creative people are more likely to [5]_____ their dreams
  Creative people = people who [6]_____ a lot or are imaginative, according to study

C Correct the one wrong word in each extract from the listening.

1. I always take these things with a gram of salt.

2. I mean, there's no worry in my mind that strong smells have an effect on how I feel.

3. With a shadow of a doubt. Sorry!

4. I wouldn't go so long as to say that, but, you know, if you think it's a good idea …

5. The judge is still out on this, but some scientists have made the claim that …

D Match 1–6 to a–f to make sentences.

1. People who are very image-
2. Most of the studies into sleep are carried out by consumer-
3. Some dreams are purely stress-
4. The study wasn't very news
5. This new sleep tracker is very user-
6. I dreamed about a ghost-

a. ☐ related.
b. ☐ conscious will often have dreams about their teeth.
c. ☐ friendly. It comes with very clear instructions.
d. ☐ like figure on a beach, talking to me in French.
e. ☐ oriented companies who want to make products designed to help us sleep more easily.
f. ☐ worthy until the results were published.

18

Do you believe everything you're told? 4.2

A Use the prompts to complete the forum comments.

 What are the worst office pranks you've had played on you?

The funniest thing that's happened to me was just last week. I arrived late for work one day and was trying to sneak into the office quietly. ¹[Little / I / know] _____ , my coworkers had taped an air horn underneath my chair, the type they use at sports matches. As soon as I sat down, it let out this huge blast. Everyone turned around and burst out laughing. ²[Never / again / I / late] _____ for work! *Philippa Evans*

I'm an office manager, and ³[rarely / my staff / play] _____ pranks on me, but on my birthday this year, they all arrived early and filled my office with balloons. I mean they literally filled it with balloons. I could barely open the door! *Lesley Drake*

Last time I went on vacation I told my coworkers that when I got back, I wanted to get a plant for my desk. ⁴[Not since / my previous job / I / work] _____ in an office with no plants. Well, when I got back, somebody said to me "I hope you like your plants" on my way in. I thought it was strange, but only when I got to my desk ⁵[I / understand] _____ . They'd planted seeds inside my keyboard and there were all these little plants growing out between the keys! *Janice Dowley*

B Rewrite the sentences using emphatic inversion. Use the words in parentheses.

1 I couldn't find my keyboard anywhere! (NOWHERE)
_____

2 I only realized I had the wrong bag after I got home. (ONLY AFTER)
_____

3 We hardly ever play April Fool's Day pranks in my country. (RARELY)
_____

4 He didn't know that we'd switched his laptop for a pizza box! (LITTLE)
_____

5 I hadn't felt so embarrassed since I'd been a teenager. (NOT SINCE)
_____

C ▶15 Complete the conversations with the correct form of these verbs. There's one extra. Listen to check.

| breathe | clog | flee | throw | wreak |

1 **A:** This weather's terrible!
B: Tell me about it. It's _____ havoc with my vacation plans!

2 **A:** Have they posted the exam results yet?
B: Yes, and you can _____ a sigh of relief. You passed!

3 **A:** You're late again.
B: I know, sorry, there was an accident that _____ the highways. I was stuck in traffic for an hour.

4 **A:** Terrible what happened downtown yesterday.
B: I know, but at least everyone managed to _____ the fire, so no one was hurt.

D **Make it personal** Complete the sentences so they're true for you.

1 Not since I was a child _____ .
2 Rarely do I _____ .
3 Only after I _____ .

19

4.3 When did you last hear something illogical?

A Read paragraph 1 of Sara's blog. Check (✓) the correct inference about her attitude. What do you think she will say next?

1. ☐ She is suspicious of a post she has read.
2. ☐ She is worried about social media stealing their content.
3. ☐ She respects the person for sharing this information.

Check it before you share it! by Sara James

"With this status, I declare that all my photos, videos, and other content belongs to me...." Scrolling through my social media page, I see, with a heavy heart, that this status is back again. Worse still, it's been posted by someone I know and respect, as if this is some clever tip-off to show us that the social media site is engaging in a major cover-up to steal ownership of all our data.

The truth is, it's a hoax. You already own all your content. The social media barons aren't some shady burglar, forcing a break-in to your page to steal all the good stuff. Yet hoaxes like this are rife on social media, and I've had enough. So should you. Let's have a crackdown on sharing false information. Here's what I suggest.

When you see a shocking "news" image that portrays something scandalous, and it doesn't sit quite right, do a reverse image search. Several sites allow you to upload an image and search the Internet to find its source. That way you can tell whether it's genuine or just some throwaway post by someone who didn't bother to check it first.

There are also plenty of fact-checking sites out there. These sites trawl the Internet for bogus stories and check their authenticity. Often you'll find that that post about the imminent takeover of a family store by some faceless multinational turns out to be just not true.

You can also just check the sources of the post yourself. If it comes from a site called something like "clicksrus.com" or "welovesunglasses.com," then you can bet your bottom dollar it's not real. Search for the story yourself. If it comes up in established newspaper sites, then it might just be authentic.

Finally, call people out when they post hoaxes as if they were true. It's important we do this if we want to prevent a complete wipeout of the truth online. But be nice about it. That's why it's called "social" media, after all. So instead of saying, "This is nonsense," you could write a comment like, "You may want to run this story by a fact-checking website first."

B Choose the correct option (a, b or c).

1. Sara thinks false posts are ...
   a rare. b common. c too long.
2. A reverse image search allows you to find out ...
   a if a photo has been altered.
   b who the people in a photo are.
   c where an image came from.
3. Fact-checking websites _____ false stories on the Internet.
   a look for b share c create
4. Which of these does Sara NOT say you can do yourself?
   a pay to find out if a story is real
   b tell if a story is false by its web address
   c see if a story is credible by looking at other places it appears
5. What does Sara ask us to do at the end of her blog?
   a tell people a story that they posted is nonsense
   b tell people a story is false if they post it
   c search for a story someone posted on a fact-checking website

C Find seven nouns / adjectives formed from phrasal verbs in the article. Match them to definitions 1–7.

1. entering a building illegally and by force _____
2. disposable _____
3. destruction _____
4. action that is taken to deal strictly with a problem or a crime _____
5. an attempt to hide the truth _____
6. a secret warning _____
7. assuming control over a company _____

D **Make it personal** Complete the sentences so they're true for you.

1. When I'm online I often _____.
2. Most social media users tend to _____.
3. Sometimes I do things which might _____.

How would you describe your personality? 4.4

A Match 1–5 to a–e to make sentences with formal relative clauses.

1 A hundred people were studied,
2 It's important that we remember the work of Professor Richards,
3 It's a well-known personality test,
4 We now have the results of the research,
5 There are hundreds of people

a   for whom this personality trait is desirable.
b   without whom the discovery wouldn't have been possible.
c   from which we can conclude that certain personality types crave attention.
d   about which many books have been written.
e   most of whom had some kind of undesirable personality trait.

B Complete the texts with these words and phrases.

> about which   whom   towards which   in which   most of whom   which

INVOLUNTARY EXPRESSION DISORDER (IED)

This is an actual condition ¹_____ people have uncontrollable emotional expressions. They might have heard that something terrible has happened to someone, ²_____ they love and care for, but all they can do is laugh uncontrollably. The condition, ³_____ very little is still known, is also called pseudobulbar affect.

PERSONALITY TRAIT OR MEDICAL DISORDER?

OPPOSITIONAL DEFIANT DISORDER (ODD)

People with this condition don't respond well to authority, ⁴_____ they can become hostile, angry, or vindictive. This isn't just the normal rejection of authority, ⁵_____ most children experience at one point or another. It goes much further than that. A person with ODD can continuously cause problems for at least six months.

ALEXITHYMIA

This is a disorder where people are simply unable to express their feelings or emotions. It affects about 10% of the population, ⁶_____ also have trouble reading the expressions of others.

C ▶16 Decide if the **bold** letter s is pronounced /s/ (S) or /z/ (Z). Listen to check.

1 A: What do you think of the idea in the article?
   B: Well, it's an interesting hypothe**sis**, but I'd take it with a grain of salt. ☐ ☐
2 A: Oh, you're *such* a kind person.
   B: Enough of your **s**arca**s**m! ☐ ☐
3 A: Do you ever u**s**e personality tests at your company? ☐
   B: Oh, yes, we make u**s**e of them all the time. ☐
4 A: What are these figures ba**s**ed on? ☐
   B: They're taken from each pha**s**e of the research we've carried out. ☐

21

4.5 Would you ever hire a former criminal?

A Number the paragraphs of the letter to a newspaper in order (1–6).

By James Hartfield

a ☐ First, there is some ¹_____ as to whether conspiracy theories actually keep the government (whom we should certainly question) in check. In fact, once they are inevitably shown to be the nonsense that they are, they give credibility to the government that denied the claims in the first place. The truth always comes out in the end.

b ☐ For all of the reasons above, I urge you to stop publishing such theories, and make sure people who push them are banned from being published in this newspaper again. It's up to us to check the facts, so let's put this nonsense to bed, once and for all.

c ☐ Many letters in this newspaper have perpetuated various ridiculous conspiracy theories of late, one of which is the suggestion that Elvis Presley is still alive and well, and has been spotted working at a gas station in the Midwest. I ²_____ believe that we need to stop peddling this nonsense and rely on the facts at hand.

d ☐ Second, ³_____ of how much individuals believe what they say, conspiracy theories can be disrespectful towards the people involved. For example, despite ridiculous ⁴_____ to the contrary, Man did actually set foot on the moon in 1969. It wasn't a staged production in the desert. No one is trying to conceal information here.

e ☐ Many would ⁵_____ that conspiracy theories provide a useful check on state power, as they force us to question what we are told in the media. While there is no denying that we should cast a critical eye (or ear) on everything we are told, there are compelling reasons not to do so by way of conspiracy theories.

f ☐ Finally, the abundance of conspiracy theories can prevent people from fact-checking stories for themselves, especially when shared on social media. Sharing a post might seem to mean putting the facts on the table. This can only lead to a general dumbing down of the population.

B Complete the letter with these words. Do you agree with James?

| argue   claims   debate   irrespective   strongly |

C Match the highlighted expressions in the letter to these definitions.
1. eventually we will see the real situation _____
2. out in the open for everyone to see _____
3. our responsibility/choice _____
4. hide the facts _____
5. make it so that someone is not allowed to do something _____

D Look back at lessons 4.1–4.5 in the Student's Book. Find the connection between the song lines and the content of each lesson.

E 🔊 17 Listen to the five question titles from the unit, and record your answers to them. If possible, compare recordings with a classmate.

5.1 Why do good plans sometimes fail?

A ▶18 Listen to Marta and Liam discussing an article about publicity stunts. True (T) or false (F)?
1 The AApass allowed you to travel as much as you wanted.
2 American Airlines expected people to fly as often as they did.
3 The CEO didn't realize his identity had been stolen until later.
4 The design of the "walkie-talkie" building made the air inside it very hot.

B ▶18 Listen again. What does each number refer to?
1 1981 _____
2 250,000 _____
3 50 million _____
4 1994 _____
5 2007 _____
6 13 _____
7 250 million _____
8 91 _____

C ▶19 Complete the extracts from the conversation. Listen to check.
1 Well, in the end, they realized it was a major _____ not to have anticipated customer reactions and decided to _____ the whole thing off.
2 It was a high-_____ plan, and one that fell flat on its face, too.
3 So his plans to demonstrate how secure the company was definitely fell _____ .
4 When they were on the _____ of completing it, they noticed a _____ .

D Choose the correct alternative to complete the conversations.
1 **A:** I'm really proud of what you've achieved since you lost your job.
   B: Thanks. It took me a while to *hold / pull* myself together, but I got there in the end.
2 **A:** So, how did the publicity event go?
   B: It fell flat on its *face / legs*. The band didn't even show up.
3 **A:** I can't believe it. After all that work, we're back to square *two / one*.
   B: I know, but at least we get to try out something new now.
4 **A:** Are you enjoying your job?
   B: Oh, yes, thanks, much better than the last place. I came this close *by / to* having a nervous breakdown there!
5 **A:** What was all that commotion in town the other day?
   B: Didn't you hear? That big clothing store had a sale and things got out of *hand / hands*. People were fighting each other to get the bargains.

E **Make it personal** Complete the sentences so they're true for you.
1 I was on the verge of _____ when _____ .
2 Recently I came this close to _____ .

5.2 Do you ever make resolutions?

A Complete the text with these words.

| aim | as | effort | given | thanks | view |

Going the extra mile

¹_____ the fact that most of us lead very busy lives, it's important to set ourselves goals intelligently, so ²_____ to ensure success. With the goal or ³_____ of making this easier, companies often tell their employees to set goals which are S.M.A.R.T. (Specific, Measurable, Achievable, Realistic, and Timely). Specific, measurable, and timely are definitely good ideas. But in an ⁴_____ to achieve great things, do we really want to set goals which are easily achievable and realistic? ⁵_____ to easy, achievable goals, we may never realize our true potential. After all, with a ⁶_____ to pushing his employees above and beyond, it was Steve Jobs who said, "We're here to put a dent in the universe."

B Match 1–5 to a–f to make sentences. There's one extra.

1 With the aim of making them easier to achieve,
2 In view of his health problems,
3 In an effort to reduce stress among employees,
4 Thanks to lower flight costs,
5 So as to lose weight,

a ☐ many people are traveling further on their vacations.
b ☐ Paul has decided to take some time off from work.
c ☐ big goals are usually broken down into smaller ones.
d ☐ I've decided to join a gym.
e ☐ the company is offering free meditation classes.
f ☐ more companies are charging higher fees.

C Circle the correct options.

It's the same every year on January 1st. We decide we're going to make a ¹*fresh / up-to-date* start and set ourselves bold New Year's resolutions. We ²*hold / get* our act together for the first month, but by February, our enthusiasm is already starting to falter. So how can we make sure we succeed and follow ³*through / on* with our plans? The first thing is to create a new habit. Unless it's a habit, you won't succeed. You don't need to completely start ⁴*new / anew*, just introduce small changes which you can keep. For example, instead of sitting down in front of the TV after dinner, why not go for a ten-minute walk? You may even end up going for a longer walk after a while. If you didn't eat very healthily last year, you don't need to completely turn the ⁵*page / book* and stick to salad. Just start by introducing healthier food into your diet. An apple a day is an easy way to do this, and it's full of healthy fiber, too. There's no need to reinvent yourself. Making small changes which become habits will help you stick ⁶*to / on* your plans.

D Make it personal Rewrite the sentences so they're true for you.

1 In an effort to save money, I've started walking to work/school.
_____

2 Thanks to playing sports, I keep in shape and stay healthy.
_____

3 With the aim of eating more healthily, I've started eating more fruit.
_____

How well do you deal with failure? 5.3

A Read the introduction to the website. Which of these things does the website NOT ask people to share?
1 an experience
2 reasons why failure is important
3 something positive that came from the experience

Online Failure Festival

Everyone hates to fail, but is it always a bad thing? We say no! In fact, we believe that failure is important to learn the things we need to know in order to succeed. What's your failure story, and what did you learn from it? Share your story with us below for the chance to win a great prize.

Last year, I entered a marathon and failed miserably. Because I've been running for years (though never as far as a marathon), I didn't think I needed to follow a special training plan or anything. A marathon really is a different beast from shorter distances, and at 20 miles in, I crashed and burned, or "hit the wall" as they say, and couldn't finish. I was devastated, and held on to this failure for a long time. I even stopped running for a while. But it was good for me in the end as it made me take stock, look at how I was training, and start again properly this time. This year, I entered a new marathon and went to great lengths to train properly. I had a great race and finished in under four hours.

Steve, Montreal

A few years ago, I had an idea for a new app which I believed could be really successful. I got together with a few of my friends, left my job, and we decided to launch it as part of a new business. To cut a long story short, it didn't do nearly as well as we expected, and, within a year, we had to close the company. Fortunately, I'm now working again at a large software company. The experience actually taught me a lot. Rather than dwell on the failure of the app, I learned a lot of things about launching a new product, which has given me new skills that I can now use on my job.

Vanda, San Francisco

I just published my first novel, after years of having it rejected by publishers. It can be really hard to face constant rejection, and there were times when I really thought I would never get it published. But I kept things in perspective. I strongly believe there can be no success without failure. The important thing is to put those failures behind you and learn from them. Now that I'm finally getting it published, it makes all the smaller failures worthwhile.

Carla, Delaware

B Read the people's comments on the website and complete 1–5 with the correct name. There's one extra comment.
1 _____ says the experience taught him / her things that are useful now.
2 _____ says the experience stopped him / her doing what he / she wanted for some time.
3 _____ says he / she would never make the same mistake again.
4 _____ thinks it's his / her own fault that he / she didn't succeed.
5 _____ thinks determination is important to succeed.

C ▶ 20 Complete the sentences with the correct form of phrases from the website. Listen to check.
1 Steve _____ the fact that he didn't finish the marathon for a long time.
2 Eventually he _____ of the situation and started training again.
3 He _____ to make sure he was properly prepared the second time.
4 Vanda didn't _____ the fact that her business failed.
5 After being rejected, Carla tried to _____ things _____ .
6 She thinks you should _____ failures _____ .

D Make it personal Complete the sentences so they're true for you.
1 I've recently gone to great lengths to _____.
2 I try not to dwell on _____.

25

5.4 Have you ever had a wrong first impression?

A Complete the social media comments with appropriate words.

Nina Blank: What's the most disastrous date you've ever been on?

Jackie Singleton:
I went to dinner recently with a really boring guy. He kept insisting on ¹_____ listening to him talking about himself.

Ryan McGuire:
I met a woman who was really nice, until she started talking about politics. She went on and on about how she was against ²_____ introducing healthcare reforms. She wouldn't let me get a word in edgewise.

Thomas Murphy:
I'm sick of ³_____ standing me up on dates. The last time, we went to watch a movie. She left "to get popcorn" and never came back.

Daniela McDonald:
It wasn't until after the date that I learned about ⁴_____ need for constant attention. We had a really nice lunch, but then later that afternoon and evening, he called me 10 times!

Landon Dawson:
She looked stunning. Fortunately, I'd made an effort and was wearing my new white shirt. I wasn't so impressed by ⁵_____ accidentally spilling orange juice down it!

B Correct the mistake in these sentences.
1 I can't stand my girlfriend is talking about her ex all the time. _____
2 I'm not happy about my parents' who complaining about my boyfriend. _____
3 Russ and Ella are so in love. It's so nice to see they always doing things together. _____
4 Where have you been? I was counting on you made me feel better about what happened today. _____
5 I'm sick of he's talking about his friends all the time. _____

C Circle the correct options.
1 **A:** Did you find someone to help you with your project in the end?
   B: Yes, I teamed up *for / with* a couple of others in my class, and we finished it in no time.
2 **A:** Did you work things *out / up* with your brother?
   B: I did. Things went well in the end, and we're friends again.
3 **A:** I was really counting *to / on* Joe to help me with my assignment, but he didn't do anything.
   B: Why don't you take the issue *up / on* with your professor? It's not fair that you should do all the work.
4 **A:** I'm really sorry I embarrassed you in front of your parents.
   B: It's OK. I'll let you *off / out*.
5 **A:** Phew! I was worried we wouldn't be able to stick *on / to* the deadline there.
   B: Me too, but your help was fantastic. I thought we'd wind *up / out* not finishing in time, but we made it. Thanks a million.

How bad are drivers where you live? 5.5

A Read the proposal. Which of these supporting arguments does Shaun Hogan NOT make?

The proposal ...
1 will make the area safer.   2 is cheap.   3 will help educate young people.

To: City Hall
From: Shaun Hogan
Subject: Proposal for community service program

Dear Ms. Wheeler:

As I'm sure you're aware, the trash problem in our local area has become quite a problem recently. Budget cuts to local services mean there simply aren't enough people to deal with it effectively, and it's taking its toll on the cleanliness of our neighborhood.

As president of the Fairtown Residents' Association, I'm writing to suggest a proposal we have discussed at length in our weekly meetings: We would like to team up with local schools to establish a community service cleaning project, involving local teenagers as part of normal school hours. This would involve classes of teenagers going out into the local community once a week for two hours to pick up trash from the streets.

¹Br_____ sp_____, it would have two goals: (1) to improve the cleanliness of the neighborhood, and (2) to involve young people in the community and teach them the importance of looking after their local area.

²Es_____, this would provide a solution to the lack of budget funds to clean the local area. ³Cl_____, the funds available at the moment aren't sufficient. ⁴Ad_____, it wouldn't completely provide a solution, but when coupled with existing services, it would make a difference. ⁵In_____, there is also the possibility of the students sorting through saleable recyclable material.

⁶Ob_____, this would provide benefits to the teenagers involved. We believe that it would be empowering for young people in the local area. It will allow them to feel part of the community, and responsible for how it looks. ⁷Fr_____, they may even wind up feeling proud of their area. This would be an important step in reducing the amount of trash they drop on the streets, too.

I hope I have managed to provide convincing arguments to why this plan will work. Please feel free to contact me if you have any questions or to discuss how to move forward with the proposal.

Sincerely,

Shaun Hogan

B Complete the proposal with the missing adverbial expressions 1–7. The first two letters are provided.

C Circle the correct options.
  1 **A:** What does your proposal *entail / turn down*?
     B: Well, the general idea is that we create a no parking zone on the main avenue.
  2 **A:** Is our proposal *rationale / airtight*?
     B: Yes, it is. It *spells out / turns down* all the different steps involved in the project.
  3 **A:** Have you *put together / re-read* that proposal yet?
     B: Yes, I have. And I'm afraid they put *it together / turned it down*.
     A: OK, well let's *spell it out / redo it* together and see if we can get it accepted.

D Look back at lessons 5.1–5.5 in the Student's Book. Find the connection between the song lines and the content of each lesson.

E 🔊 21 Listen to the five question titles from the unit, and record your answers to them. If possible, compare recordings with a classmate.

6 » 6.1 Do you still read paper books?

A ▶22 Listen to part of a webinar on how to be a successful content writer. Number the topics a–d in the order they're mentioned.

a ☐ writing original content
b ☐ writing different types of content
c ☐ publicizing your content
d ☐ finding out information to support what you say

B ▶22 Listen again and choose the correct option (a, b, or c).

1 Writing good content is important because …
  a nowadays people have a lot of choice about what they decide to read.
  b it's difficult to choose an interesting topic to write about.
  c it's difficult to compete with traditional books and journals.
2 "Listicles" are …
  a articles about a particular group of people.
  b things we write to help us remember to do things.
  c articles with a number in the titles.
3 You can check if information in an article is true by …
  a reading it carefully for any contradictions.
  b crossing out incorrect facts.
  c finding the same information in a number of other sources.
4 If your writing style is original …
  a the way you say things will be less important than what you say.
  b people will know who's written it.
  c it will be popular.
5 A social media presence is important to …
  a demonstrate what you can write to the right people.
  b let people know you are looking for work.
  c look for ideas to include in your own work.

C ▶23 Complete the extracts from the webinar with the correct form of these phrasal verbs. Listen to check.

| bring out | cross out | pick out | point out | wear out | work out |

1 Being a successful content writer means creating stunning content which people will _____ to read.
2 Today, I'm going to show you how to write content that _____ the best of your work.
3 Successful content writers are able to _____ how to write in the appropriate style for the medium.
4 Opinion pieces, on the other hand, are often persuasive and well-researched, _____ facts that support your argument.
5 You might even want to delete the fact. You can just _____ it _____ and start again.
6 Once you've realized, you'll never _____ your welcome.

D Make it personal Write your answers to the questions.

1 Which do you prefer to do: work out the meaning of new words in a text yourself, or look them up? Why?

_____

2 What or who brings out the best in you? In what way?

_____

3 Describe a favorite item of clothing that's worn out but you still wear it.

_____

Do you ever watch dubbed movies? 6.2

A Circle the correct adverbials.

The future of movies

Developments in technology over the last thirty years have transformed the way we watch movies. But what's in store for the future? ¹*Unless / As long as* you hate watching movies, you'll find some of the developments that are just around the corner very exciting.

First of all, there's immersive audio, or 3D sound. This enables producers to place sounds at specific places around the movie theater, ²*in case / even if* the speakers are in different locations in different theaters. And full immersion doesn't just apply to audio, either. Many studios are working towards true 3D movies, so that you don't look at a screen, but see the action going on all around you. But don't worry. There will still be "traditional" options available ³*whether or not / in case* you think that's too much.

And why stop at 3D? Some movie theaters will be able to offer 4D, ⁴*as long as / unless* they have the right equipment. So, for example, when it starts raining on screen, small jets will spray water at you. Perhaps not everyone's idea of fun! But ⁵*even if / whether or not* you like these changes, they are certain to change the way we watch movies.

B Complete the conversations with adverbials from **A**.

1 **A:** I'm not sure about true 3D. Where would you know where to look?
  B: Yes, you'd be constantly looking around _____ you missed something. Sounds tiring.
2 **A:** I like the idea of true 3D, _____ it's not a horror movie.
  B: Exactly, can you imagine zombies creeping up behind you?!
3 **A:** I love the idea of 4D effects.
  B: You do? I wouldn't go to the movies _____ I was wearing waterproof clothing!
4 **A:** I'm not sure I like the idea of these innovations. They don't sound very relaxing.
  B: Yes, but _____ you like them, you have to admit they're very interesting.
5 **A:** Do you go to the movies a lot?
  B: No, and I'll always prefer watching at home, _____ these innovations happen.

C ▶24 Complete the comments about a movie with these words. There's one extra. Listen to check.

| curiosity | money | patience | sheer habit | sync | the theater | 10 |

> 1 It was so boring, I walked out of _____ half way through.
> 2 I'd never heard of this movie before, so just went to see it out of _____ . I'm glad I did. It was amazing.
> 3 It's a good movie, but the subtitles and sound were a bit out of _____ , which made it difficult to follow at times.
> 4 Nine out of _____ of this director's movies are a flop. This was the 1 out of 10, fortunately.
> 5 It takes a long time for the action to start, and I nearly ran out of _____ . But then it did, and I'm glad I waited.
> 6 I often choose action movies just out of _____ , so this time I decided to watch a comedy, and really enjoyed it.

D **Make it personal** Complete the sentences so they're true for you.

1 I never go to the movies unless _____ .
2 I like watching movies at home as long as _____ .

6.3 Who are your favorite authors?

A Read the article. Match topics 1–6 to paragraphs a–e. There's one extra topic.

1. ☐ how he started writing children's books
2. ☐ what the writer finds fascinating about Roald Dahl
3. ☐ his legacy
4. ☐ the idea for a famous children's book
5. ☐ his books that were made into movies
6. ☐ some of Roald Dahl's earlier jobs

Roald Dahl *A story of a life*

a. I've always loved reading Roald Dahl's stories, not only as a child but also more recently again as an adult. It always amazed me how one man could create such vivid worlds of imagination with such universal appeal. And now, standing here in the Roald Dahl museum, set in a small village about thirty minutes from London, where he lived and wrote the stories, I'm starting to realize how he was able to do so.

b. They say you should write about what you know, even if it doesn't seem that interesting to you. Well, Roald Dahl certainly had a wealth of source material. Before becoming a writer, he worked as an explorer for an oil company, a World War II fighter pilot (fighting in such major battles as the Battle of Athens), a diplomat, and an intelligence officer. In fact, it was during his time as an officer that he wrote his first published work, *A Piece of Cake*, about his wartime adventures.

c. His first children's book (the genre he is most famous for) was called *The Gremlins*, and was about badly-behaved mythical creatures who bustled about, making the lives of World War II fighter pilots difficult in any way they could. But most of his inspiration for his children's stories came from his own childhood. When he was eight, he and four of his friends were punished for putting a dead mouse in a jar of gobstoppers (a popular candy in the UK with children in the 1920s) in the local candy store. He and his friends called this "The Great Mouse Plot of 1924." He would later write about this candy in his story *The Everlasting Gobstopper*.

d. Perhaps the greatest inspiration from his childhood came from his time at Repton School for Boys. Situated nearby was the Cadbury's Chocolate Factory. Occasionally they would send samples of chocolate for the boys at the school to test. Roald Dahl dreamed of the day he would design a new chocolate bar that would impress Mr. Cadbury. Later on this was the inspiration for him to write *Charlie and the Chocolate Factory*.

e. In later life, he went on to write some of the most famous children's stories of all time. Even now, over 25 years after his death, his stories are as magical and popular as ever.

B Read the article again. True (T) or false (F)?

1. The writer couldn't understand how Roald Dahl could be so imaginative before he visited the museum.
2. Roald Dahl's first children's story was about a cake.
3. Roald Dahl's inspiration for his children's stories only came from his own childhood.
4. He wrote a story about a candy shop when he was only eight years old.
5. Cadbury's Chocolate Factory would involve the boys at his school in chocolate production.
6. The writer thinks Roald Dahl's stories still have universal appeal today.

C Circle the correct option.

1. Timothy leaned forward and *sniffed / fidgeted* the mug – the warm, sweet smell of chocolate.
2. Feeling nervous and not knowing what to do with her hands, Lucinda *clasped / cocked* them behind her back.
3. I tried to remain calm, but my *bustling / twitching* eye gave me away.
4. As she looked towards me, her eyelids *fidgeted / fluttered*, and she smiled.
5. Sit still George, and stop *fidgeting / fluttering*!

What do you think of graffiti art? 6.4

A 🔊25 Complete the conversation with the missing auxiliaries. Listen to check.

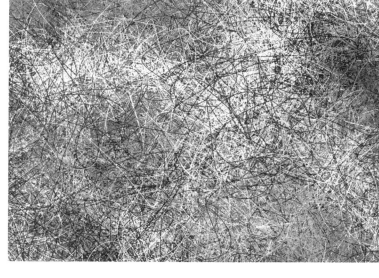

LISA: Have you seen that exhibit at the Museum of Modern Art yet?

RAFAEL: No, and I really ¹_____ not like modern art. It's just so pointless and easy.

LISA: I know what you mean. It ²_____ seem like that sometimes, doesn't it? But there's often more to it than meets the eye. You just have to be open to it.

RAFAEL: I ³_____ open to it! So, tell me what you mean.

LISA: OK, well take Jackson Pollock's work, for example. At first, his paintings just look like random blotches of paint.

RAFAEL: They ⁴_____ look like that, yes.

LISA: But, actually, his work contains what are called "fractals," which are infinitely complex mathematical patterns. He created them by very carefully dripping paint on the canvas. And they've been analyzed by computer software to show this. I bet you weren't aware of that.

RAFAEL: Wow, I ⁵_____ know that! Maybe I'll go and check out this exhibit after all.

B Replace the underlined words in each statement with auxiliaries as rejoinders.
1 I really <u>liked</u> the exhibit, even though I didn't say so. _____
2 Karla<u>'s been</u> working really hard lately. You just haven't seen her. _____
3 Wow, James <u>likes</u> graffiti art, doesn't he? _____
4 My mom<u>'s open</u> to me studying art at college, though she'd prefer it if I studied business. _____
5 You really <u>hated</u> the show, didn't you? _____

C Use the clues to complete the word puzzle with the adjectives from **7D** in the Students' Book. Guess the word in the shaded boxes.

1 interesting and full of variety
2 boring
3 very good, especially in an unexpected way
4 involving lots of new ideas
5 very strange
6 different from anything before
7 exciting, full of life
8 without new ideas, repetitive
9 makes you want to do something

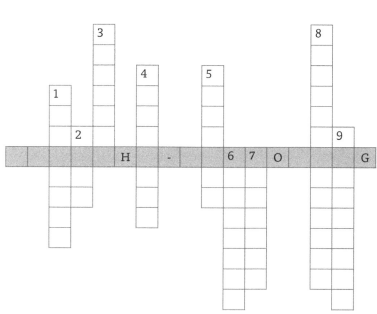

31

6.5 Are musicals popular where you live?

A Read the book review. Which of these adjectives would the writer NOT use to describe the story?

☐ bizarre ☐ funny ☐ thought-provoking

THE HUMANS Matt Haig

Science fiction is a crowded genre, with many different books available. ¹☐ And it does this with a somewhat absurd, but at the same time believable, storyline.

The plot centers around Professor Andrew Martin of Cambridge University. ²☐ However, he's not alone, and by no means the first to have done so. His actions are observed by a remote alien race, observing him from afar, one of whom is sent to earth to assassinate him. The alien race, believing that humans are incapable of handling such knowledge responsibly, feels that unless this matter is dealt with swiftly, the results will be disastrous.

The alien being tasked with the mission arrives on Earth bewildered and disgusted by humans, but as he comes to learn more about them, gradually learns to love them. ³☐

I won't say any more about what happens in order not to spoil the experience for you. ⁴☐ It's written with a broad audience in mind and is full of suspense, a real page-turner. At the end of the book, the "alien" gives us a list of 87 pieces of advice, gleaned from his experience during his time on our planet. Though meant to be humorous, it is at the same time insightful and moving, with such gems as, "Don't think you know, know you think."

I wholeheartedly recommend *The Humans* to anyone who not only enjoys an amusing read, but also enjoys something that can inspire all of us to think deeply about what it is to be human.

B Complete the review with extracts a–d.

a Alone in his office one night, he discovers the secret of prime numbers, a mathematical anomaly which allows him to unlock the secrets of the universe.

b Haig is a master at describing the human race in terms of both positive and negative traits, and you are left reassessing everything you thought you knew about what it is to be human.

c What I will say is that this book is a hilarious read, and contains colorful and insightful descriptions of human behavior from start to finish.

d What's really unique about this book, though, is the perspective it has on our everyday lives, viewed from an outsider.

C Match techniques 1–4 to extracts a–d in **B**.

1 ☐ praising the author
2 ☐ using descriptive adjectives
3 ☐ contrasting the book with others like it
4 ☐ offering plot details

D Look back at lessons 6.1–6.5 in the Student's Book. Find the connection between the song lines and the content of each lesson.

E ▶ 26 Listen to the five question titles from the unit, and record your answers to them. If possible, compare recordings with a classmate.

7.1 What are our most important years?

A ▶27 Listen to a podcast where people share their most important milestones. Choose the correct option (a, b, or c).

Scott

Adriana

Darrell

Martha

1 What does Scott say about having a baby?
   a It was more important than being ambitious.
   b It was the first time someone else was more important to him than himself.
   c It prevented him from going to college.
2 What was the most difficult thing about the situation Adriana describes?
   a applying for jobs and not getting them
   b working hard
   c accepting the situation
3 What does Darrell say about his life now?
   a He misses working.
   b He does more now than when he was working.
   c He needs to take more control of his situation.
4 Why was it such a shock for Martha to live abroad?
   a People weren't very nice to her.
   b She hadn't realized she'd have to learn a new language.
   c She'd never traveled before.

B ▶27 Listen again. Who says the following things?
1 It took me a long time to **come to terms with** the situation. _____
2 … and I decided I had to **take charge** of my situation. _____
3 In the end, I really felt like I **came of age** during that time. _____
4 … and see how far I'd **gotten off track**. _____
5 … all of a sudden **the stakes were higher**. _____
6 But I **made it through** the hard times. _____

C Match the **bold** expressions in B to meanings 1–6.
1 reach adulthood _____
2 take control _____
3 gone in the wrong direction _____
4 there's more at risk _____
5 accept _____
6 survived _____

D Complete the expressions with these animals.
1 After years of working in the city, I decided to get out of the _____ race and move to the country.
2 If I'd known my blog post was going to open such a big can of _____, I'd never have written it.
3 I'm really sorry, but I think I may have let the _____ out of the bag about your engagement.
4 I was going to start my own business last year, but I _____ out at the last minute.
5 Have you heard? Melissa and David are going to have a baby. I heard it straight from the _____ mouth!

E **Make it personal** Describe a situation when you took the bull by the horns.

_____

_____

33

7.2 Would you like to live to be 100?

A Complete the predictions with the future perfect simple or continuous form of the verbs in parentheses.

Who will live to be 100 in 2050? No one knows for sure exactly, but here are some predictions.

Centenarians:

- ¹ _____ (get) married at some time in their lives. 93% of those who live to be 100 today have lived as part of a married couple.
- ² _____ (acknowledge) by their country. In the UK, centenarians receive a telegram from the queen. In Ireland, they receive a "Centenarian Bounty" of €2,540, and in Japan, they receive a silver cup and a letter.
- ³ _____ (have) children later in life. Woman who have had children in their 40s are four times as likely to live to 100.
- ⁴ _____ (exercise) every day for many years. They also ⁵ _____ (not be) overweight.
- ⁶ _____ (live) most of their lives in France or Japan. Statistics show that these two countries produce the highest number of centenarians.

B Correct the mistakes in these sentences. One sentence is correct.
1. By the time they retire, the average American will have been earned 1.4 million dollars.
2. I will have been traveling to over 50 countries by the time I'm 70.
3. Statistics show that 40% of the workplace will have been forced into early retirement through illness.
4. The new retirement laws won't have been coming into effect by the time she retires.
5. Next year, Bill will have been worked for 50 years, and he shows no signs of wanting to stop yet!
6. By 2025, it's expected that more money will have allocated to services for the elderly.

C ▶ 28 Circle the correct options. Listen to check.
1. A: How long has Rita been with us?
   B: At the end of the year, she *will have been working / will have been worked* here for 30 years.
   A: Really? We should get her a present or something.
2. A: Do you think you'll still be working in 10 years?
   B: I hope not! I *will have been retired / will have retired* by then if I have enough money saved.
3. A: Have you heard the news about the job layoffs?
   B: Again? That means that by the end of the year, more than 2,000 people *will have been fired / will have fired*!
   A: I know, either that, or they *will be forced / will have been forced* into early retirement.
4. A: We *will have saved / will have been saving* $5,000 by the end of the year.
   B: Really? We should do something nice to celebrate.
5. A: It says here that by the end of the financial crisis, more than twenty thousand people *will have been losing / will have lost* their jobs.
   B: Oh, that's sad.

D **Make it personal** Rewrite the sentences so they're true for you.
1. I will have retired by the time I'm 50.

   _____

2. When I'm 90, I will have been working all my life.

   _____

Do babies ever surprise you? 7.3

A Read the article. Does the writer think we are born honest or dishonest?

Are we born HONEST?

A Aw, look at that sweet, innocent face. Fresh to the world, and as yet not corrupted by the evils of the world around them, it's difficult to believe that babies are capable of anything other than honesty. Surely they don't even have the mental capacity at that age to lie? Well, if recent research is anything to go by, it appears that may not be true.

B Until now, there has been a general consensus that we are born honest, and it's not until we come into contact with the wider world that we develop the ability to bend the truth. What's more, we don't develop the language or [1]_____ expressions needed in order to lie until the age of four. Lying is a complex cognitive procedure, an [2]_____ decision based on the experience we gain in our [3]_____ lives, with which we need to have an understanding of what's right or wrong.

C Current research, however, has blown that idea out of the water. It seems lying is an [4]_____ trait. A recent study showed that babies as young as six months old use fake crying and pretend laughing to get what they want. Lying is actually a [5]_____ ability babies develop in the [6]_____ stages of life. A [7]_____ sense of what's right and wrong, it appears, doesn't come until later in childhood. This is why fairy tales and children's stories with a moral are so important.

D What's more, babies don't just lie, but go as far as to manipulate to get what they want. They'll scream, hit themselves, and even hold their breath until they pass out – a condition known as a "breath-holding spell." This might seem like an [8]_____ transaction, but to babies, it's a [9]_____ deal. If they want it, why can't they have it?

E All of this seems to point towards the conclusion that humans are inherently born dishonest. Rather than shield children from the reality of life to prevent them from being "corrupted," it's, therefore, more important to educate them from an early age as to what's right and what's wrong.

B Match summary sentences 1–6 to paragraphs A–E. There's one extra sentence.
1 ☐ Babies are actually capable of lying.
2 ☐ Babies will even do more than just lie to achieve things.
3 ☐ We think babies are born honest and later develop the ability to lie.
4 ☐ Babies don't actually know how to be honest.
5 ☐ It's important to teach young children a sense of morality.
6 ☐ Babies look honest and unable to lie.

C Complete the collocations in the article with these adjectives.

| crucial | daily | early | evolutionary | fair | facial | informed | rudimentary | unfair |

7.4 Do you seem younger or older than you are?

A Order the words in italics to complete the cleft sentences in the text.

Achieving the impossible

¹*not / that / are / old / you / it's / how* determines what you are able to achieve. And these people have proved it. Take Teiichi Igarashi, for example. At the ripe old age of 100, he became the first centenarian to climb Mount Fuji in Japan. ²*time / it / the / wasn't / that / first* he'd done it, either. It was his 12th ascent!

³*people / who / just / not / it's / young* can set world records, either. In May 2016, ⁴*100 year-old / who / was / Ida Keeling / it* set a new world record of 1:17:33 in the 60-meter dash for U.S. women over age 90.

Some people say you can't teach an old dog new tricks, but the case of Nola Ochs goes to show that ⁵*age / your / it's / that / not* stops you from learning. At 95, she became the oldest person to attain a college degree. As if that wasn't remarkable enough, at 98 she went on to graduate with a Master's degree!

It just goes to show that time is no obstacle to what we can achieve when we really apply ourselves. ⁶*yourself / it's / that / belief / in / only / your* holds you back, not your age.

Ida Keeling

Nola Ochs

1 _____   4 _____
2 _____   5 _____
3 _____   6 _____

B Rewrite these people's opinions on the article using a cleft sentence.

1 "I only feel respect when I see people's achievements."
   It's _____ when I see their achievements.
2 "Your attitude determines what you can do – at any age."
   It's _____ what you can do – at any age.
3 "I'm most impressed by their perspective on life."
   It's _____ impresses me most.
4 "These people have a belief in themselves."
   It's _____ these people have.
5 "Their achievements leave me speechless."
   It's _____ me speechless.

C ▶29 Complete the text with these words. Listen to check.

| act | conform | hand | heart | pushing | wise |

Everyone tells me I should ¹_____ my age, but why should I? OK, I'm ²_____ 90, but that doesn't mean I should ³_____ to expectations. I want to make the most of the time I have left, and I want to gain first-⁴_____ experience in all the things I've always dreamed about. When I was younger, I was far too practical, you see. People said I was "⁵_____ beyond my years" but, to tell you the truth, I wish I'd been a bit more adventurous, made a few more mistakes. Well, I might be old now, but I'm young at ⁶_____, and if it keeps me healthy and fit, then all the better!

D **Make it personal** Complete the sentences so they're true for you.

1 It was my parents who _____.
2 It's _____ that impresses me most.

36

What would your ideal job be? 7.5

A Read the job-application letter. Which of the following does James not have a lot of?

☐ qualifications ☐ experience ☐ skills

Director of Studies — • — Fast track English   September 30

Dear Sir or Madam,

I am writing in ¹_____ to your job opening for an English teacher, as advertised online on September 24. I believe I am highly ²_____ to the position, and am attaching a recent copy of my résumé.

Having graduated last year with a Master's in Linguistics, I am eager to find full-time employment as an English teacher. As you will ³_____ on my résumé, a large part of my degree consisted of practice teaching, for which I achieved high ratings. I, therefore, believe my knowledge and experience to date would be a perfect ⁴_____ for the position you have available.

While teaching as part of my graduate program, I was told by my professors that I have a dynamic presence in the classroom, and I am attentive to my students' needs. I communicate well, and I believe I am receptive to new ideas. I am also proactive in helping students reach their full potential. Before starting college, I worked part-time as a receptionist at a small private language school. My responsibilities there included registering new students, answering questions, and maintaining up-to-date records. In this ⁵_____ , I was also able to gain valuable insights into the running of a school.

While I am aware my teaching experience is not yet extensive, I am no stranger to the classroom. I am also responsive to feedback and have a good knowledge of teaching theory, which I believe I will be able to convert into practical day-to-day teaching solutions.

I hope you will give my application careful ⁶_____ . Thank you very much in advance.
Sincerely,

James Tuffnal

James Tuffnal

B Complete the letter with these words. There's one extra.

| capacity   consideration   fit   response   responsibility   see   suited |

C Match the highlighted words in the letter to definitions 1–4.

1 ready to accept new suggestions _____
2 wants to create solutions _____
3 able to pay close attention _____
4 energetic and exciting _____

D Circle the correct option.

1 I wonder if I could *possibly / probably* borrow your tablet for an hour or so.
2 **A:** I hope I'm not *disturbing / interrupting*.
   B: No, it's fine. How can I help you?
3 Ah, Michael. Come in. Would you be so *kind / lovely* as to close the door?
4 I had an idea for the marketing campaign that I wanted to *run / walk* by you.
5 **A:** So that's my idea for the budget. *Would / Should* it be OK if I went ahead?
   B: I'll need to check some of those numbers, but I think they'll be OK.

E Look back at lessons 7.1–7.5 in the Student's Book. Find the connection between the song lines and the content of each lesson.

F ▶ 30 Listen to the five question titles from the unit, and record your answers to them. If possible, compare recordings with a classmate.

37

8 » 8.1 What makes a restaurant special?

A ▶31 Listen to a radio interview with Cameron Mathis from the Movement Against Patronizing Advertisements (MAPA). Which four things does he not like to see in advertising?

1 ☐ images used to represent a company or product in a childish way
2 ☐ online ads
3 ☐ people with childish faces
4 ☐ commercials aimed at children
5 ☐ childish music
6 ☐ false claims about products

B ▶31 Listen again. True (T) or false (F)?

1 MAPA is against all advertising.
2 Cameron thinks some ads could be mistaken for children's programs.
3 He thinks childish ads make people less critical.
4 He thinks children should be involved in making decisions about paying bills.
5 MAPA wants to take these companies to court.
6 He believes we all have to protest against this type of advertising.

C Match phrases 1–5 from the listening to what they refer to (a–e). One matches to two items.

1 taking the Internet by storm
2 take a stand against
3 take offense at
4 take the blame for
5 take matters into their own hands

a ☐ commercials that treat us like children
b ☐ companies that use childish advertising
c ☐ good ads
d ☐ people in general (what they need to do)
e ☐ the "dumbing-down" of society

D Complete the conversations with these words. There's one extra.

| apologize   enough   insult   matters   top |

1 **A:** Oh, I hate this ad!
   B: Me too! And to make _____ worse, it's on all the time!
2 **A:** Have you seen that commercial for orange juice?
   B: No, why?
   A: It's awful. They have this little singing band of oranges. On _____ of that, they all shouted "Juiced!" at the end, in these really childish voices.
3 **A:** I'm not sure I liked Neil's idea for our new poster campaign.
   B: I know, right? Absolutely terrible. As if that were not _____ , I think the boss actually liked it.
4 **A:** I'm thinking about going to that new Italian restaurant advertised in the local paper.
   B: I wouldn't if I were you. We went there last week. The service was terrible, and our food was cold when it arrived. To add _____ to injury, they charged us extra for water!

E Make it personal Answer the questions.

1 What types of things do you take offense at? _____
2 When did you last take a stand against something? _____
3 In what situations would you take matters into your own hands? _____
4 Describe something that is currently taking the Internet by storm. _____

Are you a demanding customer? 8.2

A Circle the correct option in the complaints.

Five ridiculous customer complaints that will make you laugh

1 Visitors to a zoo were disappointed when the animals looked sad. They insisted the zookeepers *make / to make* the animals smile.

2 After going on a hot-air balloon trip and feeling utterly terrified, one customer said it was essential *for / that* the organizers display a sign to warn people they shouldn't get on if they're afraid of heights.

3 One visitor to Disneyland demanded the company to *refund / refund* his ticket after complaining it was "too touristy."

4 A movie-goer, after watching Titanic, complained online that she wished the story *weren't / aren't* so predictable.

5 A vacationer in Greece suggested a resort *looks / look* into its discriminatory policies after reading a sign which said "No hairdressers on site." She felt discriminated against because she was a hairdresser.

B Rewrite the sentences to make them more formal. Use the subjunctive.

1 You need to listen to your customers. It's important _____ .
2 I want your company to give me a refund! I insist _____ .
3 You really must make customers aware of your policy first. It's essential _____ .
4 I'm sad this dress is so expensive. I wish _____ .
5 You should be more polite when taking orders. I suggest _____ .
6 I want you to give me a bigger seat! I demand _____ .

C 🔊 32 Complete the text with the correct subjunctive form of these verbs. Listen to check.

| be   give   not be   know   reassess   write |

👎 How to complain effectively 👎

Some people are very good at complaining when they receive bad service and know exactly how to get what they want in terms of compensation. Here's what to do.

Firstly, it's essential you ¹_____ what you want to achieve. If you're going into a complaint without knowing what action you want taken, then I suggest you ²_____ what it is you're looking for.

When you complain, it's important you ³_____ or go in person. Don't use the phone, as it's unlikely you'll be put through to the right person. Also, the company can hang up. If a visit doesn't work, try social media. Most companies today secretly wish social media ⁴_____ in existence, as it's an effective way to voice your complaint to the world.

It's critical that you ⁵_____ polite at all times. This will ensure the other person is on your side and will want to help you – and that's half the battle.

Finally, don't make ridiculous demands such as "I insist you ⁶_____ me a free vacation." Give the company something to work with, and it's more likely to find an acceptable solution.

D **Make it personal** Complete the sentences so they're true for you.

1 I wish most companies _____ .
2 If I receive bad service, I insist _____ .
3 When complaining, I think it's essential _____ .

8.3 What are the worst aspects of air travel?

A Read and complete the article with headings a–e. There's one extra.
- a It's not a bed!
- b Don't hog the space!
- c Take it with you when you leave!
- d Be quiet!
- e Keep your shoes on!

Nightmare passengers

All too often we hear complaints about airlines – delayed flights, not enough legroom, and poor-quality food – we wish it weren't like this, but it's the reality of air travel today. The fact that most airlines in recent years have gone to great lengths to cut costs hasn't really helped matters, either. But is it just passengers who suffer? We took it upon ourselves to interview 100 airline employees to find out what their biggest gripes are.

1 ____ Most everyone we spoke to complained about passengers who exposed their bare – and often smelly – feet. One flight attendant told us about a passenger who went the extra mile in order to get comfortable by poking his feet in the space between the two seats in front – while everyone was eating! The people in front got a nasty shock, and luckily Judy, a seasoned flight attendant, was there and saw to it that he stopped. "It's not uncommon to see feet in the air, on tables, in the aisles," says Judy. "People will move mountains to give their dirty feet an airing."

2 ____ Some people simply refuse to put their small bags under the seat in front. "This happens at least once every flight," said Michael, a flight attendant for a leading American airline. "We have to explain that they take up valuable overhead space, and that it's essential we leave it free for bigger bags. However, more often than not, the customer will insist on leaving the bag there, even after we go out of our way to find a better place for it."

3 ____ "You wouldn't believe what people leave behind," continues Michael, when we ask him about messy travelers. From chewing gum, to dirty diapers! Some people seem to treat the plane as a giant, flying trash can, leaving the exhausted flight attendants to clean up after them.

4 ____ While these examples aren't a direct problem for airline staff, they cause a lot of aggravation. While most of us accept the need for a little comfort on a long-haul flight, there are some passengers who feel that even for a short, thirty-minute hop, it's acceptable to slam their seat back straight after takeoff. Worse still, the passenger sitting behind might take it from there and purposely kick the other passenger's seat, causing arguments and sometimes violence, which you really don't want when you're at 15,000 feet.

B Circle the correct option to complete the sentences about the article.
1. Cheaper air fares have made problems for passengers *better / worse*.
2. One passenger exposed his feet to others during *meal time / takeoff*.
3. People put small bags in the overhead compartment even when *there isn't space / the flight attendant asks them not to*.
4. Some people leave *used baby products / drinks* on their seats when they leave.
5. The writer believe it's *unacceptable / acceptable* to recline your seat on a flight with a long duration.

C Complete the statements with a word from the article.
1. Even though our seats were booked separately, the flight attendant went to great _____ to ensure we could sit together.
2. The guy sitting next to me took it _____ himself to offer me his vegetarian meal.
3. The flight attendant _____ to it that I had enough space for my bag in the overhead compartment.
4. The woman sitting next me went out of her _____ to make sure she had full use of the arm rest!
5. After showing you to the gate, the airline staff will _____ it from there and guide you onto the airplane.

Have you ever borrowed money? 8.4

A Complete the text with these words and phrases.

> as useful as   for all the   however   much as   whatever

Avoid sorrow when you borrow

If you're thinking of borrowing money, it's important you do so wisely in order to avoid falling into the debt trap. ¹_____ amazing offers banks and credit companies provide, repaying the loan should always be your most important consideration.

- First of all, know the terms. ²_____ the deal may be, always, always read the small print. If it's a credit card, are there any annual fees? If it's a loan, and it's interest-free for the first six months, what will the interest be after that? ³_____ attractive the money may seem at first, is your financial situation really likely to improve after that time?

- Secondly, seek advice from an independent source. ⁴_____ loan companies might be when "selling" you the loan, they want you to borrow from them at the end of the day. There are numerous places that offer free advice, both online and in person. Run the terms by them first.

- Finally, do your math. ⁵_____ a $50 monthly repayment appears manageable, work out how much you'll end up repaying in total. It might not look so attractive after all.

B Match 1–5 to endings a–e to make sentences.

1 For all the help the bank
2 As useful as credit cards
3 Whatever interest rate they
4 However helpful the bank
5 As much as you

a ☐ might be, you still need to get independent advice, too.
b ☐ may be, it's important you keep track of how much you spend.
c ☐ want to borrow the money, make sure you can really afford it.
d ☐ offers, it just wants your money.
e ☐ might offer, you'll still pay back a lot more than you borrowed.

C Use the clues to complete the crossword with words related to money.

ACROSS
1 Business was good last year. We made a _____ of $120,000.
3 Can you believe that café? They wanted to _____ me $25 for a sandwich!
5 I need to _____ some money so I can buy a new car.
6 A: But I thought it was cheaper than that?
   B: The price doesn't include _____ .

DOWN
2 I've just heard that I'm going to _____ money from a long-lost relative.
4 We can offer you a _____ with an interest rate of 18%.

8.5 What was the last complaint you made?

A Read the letter of complaint and choose the correct summary.

1 The family's bags were damaged.
2 The family's bags were lost.
3 The family's bags arrived late.

Mr. Paul Gaines
Customer Service Director

Dear Mr. Gaines:

I am writing with reference to a recent experience I had when flying on your airline from San José del Cabo to Los Angeles. I have already spoken to your customer-service representatives to try and ¹*rectify / reason* the problem by phone, but to no ²*answer / avail*.

On December 24 last year, I traveled with my family to San José del Cabo, for our annual vacation. We were supposed to connect in Phoenix, Arizona with a two-hour layover, but when we arrived at LAX airport for our flight, we were told that our flight had been delayed by three hours, and that we would make a later connection to Mexico. We were also told that our baggage would arrive safely on the later flight. Notwithstanding the ³*information / fact* that we were given this assurance by your ground crew, when we arrived in San José del Cabo, our luggage was not there. When I spoke to staff in the airport to try to ⁴*repeat / resolve* the issue, I was told that it would be delivered the next morning to our hotel.

However, it actually took ten days to arrive because it had been left at the airport for most of that time. I would have been ⁵*happy / delighted* to come and collect it, but your staff told me on the phone repeatedly that this was not company policy. As I'm sure you can appreciate, this ruined our vacation, which we spent primarily shopping for new clothes.

While I understand that this is a busy time of year for you, especially at this destination, this level of service is nonetheless unacceptable. I trust that you will seek to reimburse me for the extra expenses I incurred. In the event that I do not receive ⁶*satisfaction / money*, I will have no choice but to consider ⁷*law / legal* action. I hope these ⁸*stairs / steps* will not be necessary.

I thank you in advance for your attention to this matter. I look ⁹*after / forward* to a response.

Sincerely yours,
Lily Weston

B Circle the correct options to complete the letter.

C Replace the underlined words in the sentences with more formal alternatives.

1 I have called you repeatedly, but to no <u>success</u>. _____
2 I hope you are able to <u>help</u> me. _____
3 I look forward to <u>an answer</u>. _____
4 <u>In spite of</u> the fact that they assured me they would call me back, they didn't. _____
5 I trust you will <u>correct</u> the matter as soon as possible. _____

D Look back at lessons 8.1–8.5 in the Student's Book. Find the connection between the song lines and the content of each lesson.

E 🔊 33 Listen to the five question titles from the unit, and record your answers to them. If possible, compare recordings with a classmate.

9.1 Would you like to be a teacher?

A Read the definition of mindfulness and choose the best summary.
1. ☐ It doesn't make our problems go away, but helps us not get stressed out by them.
2. ☐ It helps us forget about our problems and focus on what's good in our lives.
3. ☐ It doesn't make our problems go away, and it can be harmful.

What is mindfulness?

Mindfulness is a way of silently focusing the mind on what we feel and what we do in our lives, in order to achieve calmness and greater clarity in the way we think. It is not intended to stop us from feeling life's pressures, but it does help us be conscious of them and cope with them in a calm, relaxed manner

B ▶34 Listen to a news story about mindfulness training at school. Match the people (1–4) with the comments about them (a–d).
1. The government
2. Grangeville Elementary
3. Some parents
4. Dorothy Quinn and the teachers

a ☐ They weren't convinced the program was a good idea at first.
b ☐ They have introduced regular mindfulness training.
c ☐ They knew the program would be beneficial from the start.
d ☐ They want to introduce regular mindfulness training.

C ▶34 Listen again and choose the correct answer (a, b, or c). Are you convinced by mindfulness?
1. Research has shown mindfulness training to have benefits for children …
   a only during class time.   b both inside and outside school.   c only on exams.
2. At first, the training was for …
   a all students.   b teachers.   c some students.
3. In a mindfulness class …
   a students do different physical activities.   b do intelligence tests.   c breathe deeply.
4. The number of children at Grangeville Elementary doing the training has …
   a grown.   b fallen.   c stayed the same.
5. The school has replaced _____ with mindfulness training.
   a physical education   b some disciplinary measures   c some subjects

D ▶35 Complete the extracts with verbs beginning with *out*. Listen to check.
1. We felt the benefits would _____ the time factor.
2. The children in the program consistently _____ those who opted out.
3. More and more children joined the program, and they now _____ considerably those who didn't take part.
4. We're also finding that their concentration levels _____ the others, too.
5. These kids _____ their immature behavior much more quickly.
6. Rather than trying to _____ the teachers and break the rules, they're being much more cooperative.

E Make it personal Change the sentences so they're true for you.
1. I think the benefits of traditional education outweigh those of trying new approaches.
2. There were some school subjects in which I outperformed my classmates.

9.2 What is alternative medicine?

A Use the prompts (1–7) to complete the passive expressions. Any surprises?

Medical myths

- "Immune boosters" ¹[believe / help / you] _are believed to help you_ get over a cold or flu. But actually, the bad effects you feel when you have a cold or flu – sneezing, coughing, runny nose – are signs that your immune system is working just fine. Any perceived "boost" to these ²[can / expect / make / you] _____ feel worse.

- Another cold and flu fallacy is that vitamin C ³[know / be / effective] _____ in treating them, right? Not so. In fact, there have been no conclusive studies to show that it works.

- Other supplements, such as multivitamin pills, ⁴[think / be / good] _____ for you, too. However, recent studies show that they are largely ineffectual. And because the supplement industry is largely unregulated, there have been no major studies into their safety.

- Drinking eight glasses of water a day ⁵[believe / hydrate / your body] _____ sufficiently. But this is based on very old medical advice, and nowadays water ⁶[known / come from / other sources] _____ , such as food. We're not walking around in a constant state of dehydration.

- For a long time in the past, sugar ⁷[report / make / kids] _____ hyperactive. But this is also not based on any conclusive studies.

B Complete the second sentence so that it has the same meaning as the first. Use passive expressions with infinitives.

1 They report that the treatments are successful.
The treatments _____ .

2 We think that humans use only 10% of their brains.
Humans _____ only 10% of their brains.

3 They believe that the new drug may be a miracle cure.
The new drug _____ a miracle cure.

4 But, in fact, we know it doesn't work.
But, in fact, it _____ .

C ▶ 36 Choose a word from each box A–C in the correct form to complete the conversation with three-word phrasal verbs. Listen to check.

A	B	C
come give go grow watch	down out (x2) through up	of for on with (x2)

TODD: What's wrong, Becky? You don't look well.
BECKY: Ugh, I think I'm ¹_____ a cold. The problem is it usually makes my asthma worse, too.
TODD: Oh, that's awful. I used to have asthma when I was a child, but I ²_____ it as I got older. Have you tried any alternative therapies?
BECKY: Oh, I've been ³_____ alternative therapies for ages now. I tried acupuncture a while back, and I went a few times, but didn't manage to ⁴_____ the total number of recommended sessions.
TODD: Yes, I know what you mean. I've tried herbal remedies for other things, but they never really worked, so I just ⁵_____ them.

D Make it personal Complete the sentences to express your own opinions.

1 Traditional medicine is believed _____ .
2 Alternative medicine is thought _____ .

What unconventional families do you know? 9.3

A Read the introduction to the article. Which sentence (1–3) best reflects the author's opinion?
1. ☐ Happy couples never fight.
2. ☐ People need to be realistic about making a long-term relationship work.
3. ☐ If you find the right person, it's easy to be happy for a long time.

What's the secret to a successful marriage?

Long-term relationships are hard work, but if you go about them in the right way, they can mean long-lasting happiness. Obviously no one expects a fairytale ¹_____, but some people are able to make it work over time. We spoke to four of those people and asked them for their best tips.

I think it's important to have a common interest and do things together. While you shouldn't have to compromise your own interests, it's good to have some you share, too. This will ensure that you spend time together, and, in the end, you'll have an overriding ²_____ to do this *with* your partner, not *without*. **Mike, 56**

It sounds obvious, but what works most for us is being open and honest. I think a lot of people have this fictitious ³_____ that if there's something bothering them, then they shouldn't trouble their significant other with it. But bottled up feelings can grow into resentment – and then you're in treacherous territory. So, if something worries you, tell him or her. You don't have to always have a lengthy ⁴_____ about it, but getting it out in the open means you can deal with it more easily and move on. **Celia, 33**

Successful couples are thought to lead happy lives, without any major crises, but that's just not true. Everyone has problems, but what's important is how you deal with them. The key is to approach problems together and in different ways. If you always do the same thing, then you'll always have the same problems. Don't make unilateral ⁵_____ – discuss the best way to solve things together. You'll find your partner becomes a valuable security ⁶_____ in times of trouble. **Darren, 38**

I know it's easy to say this, but when you're looking for a prospective ⁷_____, don't settle for anyone who treats you as anything less than special. Before I met my hubby, I dated a few guys who were wonderful at first, but, after a while, started to criticize me rather than just love me for who I am. In those early days, watch how they treat other people – their parents, salesclerks, coworkers. That will show you how they'll treat you in years to come. If they're not kind, then they're not up to the task of being your life companion, let alone child ⁸_____. **Angela, 28**

B Read the rest of the article, ignoring the blanks. Match the possible situations 1–4 to each person.
1. They were having financial problems, so decided to sell their car and use public transportation to get to work instead. _____
2. Both members of this couple have their own set of friends, but on Sundays they're going biking in the park together. _____
3. She wanted to go back to college to get a degree. He told her he thought she'd do really well. _____
4. He was worried that she was spending a lot of time with a coworker. He spoke to her about it, and she told him they were just working on a project together for six weeks. _____

C Re-read the article. True (T) or false (F)? Whose advice did you think was best?
1. Mike thinks it's difficult to find time to do things together.
2. Celia doesn't like to trouble her partner with small things that worry her.
3. She thinks you don't have to spend a lot of time talking about how you feel.
4. Darren thinks relationships can be difficult, and you should find a way of solving problems by yourself.
5. Angela thinks some partners might treat you differently over time.

D Complete the article with these words.

| belief | blanket | choices | discussion | desire | ending | mate | rearing |

45

9.4 How often do you work out?

A Circle the correct options.

Pablo's story

Two years ago, I was horrendously overweight, eating badly, and feeling depressed. My doctor urged me ¹*to change / change* my lifestyle, but I had no idea where to start. My weight prevented me ²*to do / from doing* anything too strenuous, such as running, but I knew I had to do something. So I went to see a nutritionist, and she had me ³*to make / make* small changes to my diet. For example, she encouraged me ⁴*to replace / from replacing* all chocolate and candy with fruit. It was hard at first, but I insisted ⁵*to keep / on keeping* at it, and gradually, I started to actually enjoy it. Eventually, the weight started coming off, and this enabled me ⁶*to start / starting* exercising. I joined a gym, and there I had a personal trainer who was great. He warned me ⁷*to do / not to do* too much, too quickly at first. But at the same time, he made me ⁸*do / to do* exercises I wouldn't have thought of doing otherwise. I really appreciated ⁹*his / he* helping me patiently like that. Since then, I've lost nearly 50 pounds, and it's helped me ¹⁰*enjoy / enjoying* life so much more.

B Correct the mistake in these sentences. One sentence is correct.
1 When I was younger, my parents dissuaded me eating too much candy. _____
2 My leg injury caused me stopping running for two months. _____
3 The gym won't let you to join until you've had a checkup with your doctor. _____
4 Schools should discourage children to eat junk food. _____
5 This new app reminds you to do exercise throughout the day. _____
6 My personal trainer discouraged me from lift too much weight at first. _____

C Complete the text with the verb form of the words in parentheses.

There's no denying that living a sedimentary lifestyle can ¹_____ (threat) our health in many different ways. Sitting at a desk all day can not only ²_____ (weak) our muscles, but also ³_____ (worse) our health in other ways, such as giving us bad posture. The problem is, with a busy work schedule, many of us just don't have the time to visit the gym every day. But you don't need to join an expensive gym in order to stay in shape and remain healthy. There are many different exercises you can do at home or at work, using only your body weight. You can ⁴_____ (soft) the blow by doing them in short intervals, spread throughout the day. And as you become more adept, there's no need to ⁵_____ (length) each workout either, but just do more intervals. You really can ⁶_____ (strength) your body this way, and, not only this, it will ⁷_____ (fresh) you up so you can stay more alert and focused while working.

Visit **deskworkouts.id** for more details about our training schedules.

No time for the gym? No problem!

D **Make it personal** Complete the sentences so they're true for you.
1 When I was young, my parents always encouraged me _____.
2 I'd love to have someone _____.
3 I wish someone had dissuaded me _____.

46

What are the pros and cons of dieting? 9.5

A Read the report. Is the writer for or against dieting overall?

A report on the pros and cons of dieting

Today's image-obsessed society puts a lot of pressure on people to lose weight and aim for a slender physique. Added to this, obesity levels have been steadily rising in many developed countries to unhealthy proportions. For these reasons, many people attempt to lose weight by dieting, following carefully-controlled plans that aim to limit the amount of calories they consume each day. There are many reasons given for doing this.

- ¹_____: Simply put, if you consume fewer calories than you use each day, you'll lose weight. Restricting the number of calories you consume by following a diet plan will enable you to do this.
- ²_____: As you begin to shed the pounds, you'll feel better about yourself and the way you look.
- ³_____: Focusing on what you put in your body every day makes you notice what you eat more, and avoid subconsciously eating when perhaps you don't really need to.
- ⁴_____: A diet plan helps you learn about what types of food contain more calories and increase your cholesterol, as well as which foods provide healthier alternatives.

Nevertheless, there are just as many reasons why following a carefully controlled diet to lose weight can be harmful. Following a strict diet can ...

- ⁵_____ only a short-term solution, which may even cause you to put more weight back on after you've achieved your "target weight."
- ⁶_____ to muscle loss, as your body looks for the energy it needs elsewhere.
- ⁷_____ an unhealthy relationship with food, as you begin to worry about everything you eat.
- ⁸_____ your metabolism, causing your body to actually store more food as fat than use it for energy.

While there are clear benefits to dieting for weight loss, changing your lifestyle and exercising regularly will be easier to maintain over time. It will also generally make you much healthier.

B Complete the report with these nouns and verbs.

Nouns: awareness   confidence   education   weight loss

Verbs: create   lead   provide   slow

C Rewrite each list from a report with a consistent style.

1. Doing regular exercise can help you ...
   - strengthen your heart.
   - weight loss.
   - keep alert and focused.

2. There are many reasons people join a gym.
   - Motivation: Getting there encourages you to actually exercise.
   - Equipment: You can use state-of-the-art equipment you don't have at home.
   - Provide a safe environment: You are monitored and trained to exercise safely.

3. People who regularly practice mindfulness ...
   - concentration at work better.
   - are generally more relaxed.
   - feel better able to deal with life's pressures.

D Circle the correct option.

1. Did I hear you *correctly / rightly*? You're on a raw-food, vegan diet?
2. Who in their right *brain / mind* would count all the calories they eat every day?
3. **A:** Gary really needs to do more exercise. He's really overweight.
   B: You should reserve *judging / judgment*. You're not so healthy yourself.

E Look back at lessons 9.1–9.5 in the Student's Book. Find the connection between the song lines and the content of each lesson.

F ⏵37 Listen to the five question titles from the unit, and record your answers to them. If possible, compare recordings with a classmate.

10 » 10.1 Why do friends drift apart?

A ▶38 Listen to Ron telling his girlfriend Eva about a friend he once had and answer the questions.
1 What was gone from Ron's house?
2 What did James do after that?

B ▶38 Listen again. Complete 1–6 with *Ron* or *James*.
1 _____ doesn't think he was a real friend.
2 _____ made his life more interesting when he arrived.
3 _____ began behaving badly towards him.
4 _____ went out of the room suddenly.
5 _____ found a new group of friends.
6 _____ felt like he had been deceived.

C ▶39 Listen to Eva describe a time she lost her friend, Judy. What do these words refer to?
1 five *They'd been friends since they were five.*
2 the need to speak _____
3 early twenties _____
4 calls _____
5 Illinois _____

D Match 1–7 to a–g to form extracts from the listening.
1 He was a breath
2 The life
3 Oh, what a
4 We went
5 Real birds
6 Our conversations always went
7 I mean, we didn't always

a ☐ of the party, you know?
b ☐ beneath the surface.
c ☐ of fresh air.
d ☐ see eye to eye …
e ☐ back a long way.
f ☐ riot he was!
g ☐ of a feather.

E Circle the correct options.

1 Do you get along with Bobby?

Not really. There's no *saying / telling* why. We've just never really hit it off.

2 Can you call Chrissie for me?

Easier *said / told* than done! She never picks up her phone.

3 Why didn't you keep in touch with Charlotte?

Truth be *said / told*, I never really wanted to.

4 I guess it goes without *saying / telling* you'll be inviting Will to your party.

Of course!

5 *Say / Tell* what you will about Beth, she's always been there for you.

You're right. She's a great friend.

Who's the oldest person you know? 10.2

A Complete the article with these words. There's one extra.

> bit   every bit   far   hardly   quite   near   the harder   whole

Making friends in old age

The older you get, ¹_____ it is to make friends. When you retire, you spend less time at work and so feel a ²_____ lot more isolated than when you were working. In reality, though, you're nowhere ³_____ as isolated as you think. There are literally thousands of other people your age who are ⁴_____ as eager to make friends as you are. And making new friends isn't ⁵_____ as difficult as you think.

Often people think that they should join clubs or take up a new hobby just to make friends. But it's worth first taking the time to consider what you really enjoy doing. Finding people with a similar outlook on life to yours is ⁶_____ easier if you do something you truly enjoy. Use your existing social network, but also look a ⁷_____ wider than that. Your friends can introduce you to other people who you might not have met otherwise.

B Complete the second sentence so it has the same meaning as the first. Use the word in parentheses.

1 If you exercise more, you'll be healthier. (THE)
_____ you'll be.
2 How old you are is important. How you feel is more important. (MUCH)
How you feel _____ .
3 Eating well is essential, and so is exercise. (JUST)
Eating well _____ .
4 Having good friends is much more beneficial than having many friends. (NOWHERE)
Having many friends _____ .
5 My brother and I used to be a bit closer than we are now. (QUITE)
My brother and I _____ .
6 Making friends face-to-face is a bit more difficult than making friends online. (SLIGHTLY)
Making friends online _____ .

C Match beginnings 1–6 to endings a–f.

1 What's the key to
2 I love seeing my friends, but while I'm studying, I try to limit myself to
3 After what Olivia said about Leon, he didn't want to
4 I'm really looking forward to
5 My grandma does a lot of charity work. She's really committed to
6 I would love to

a ☐ going out once a week.
b ☐ being happy when you retire?
c ☐ speak to her any more.
d ☐ live to be 100!
e ☐ helping others in her old age.
f ☐ retiring, I've had enough of work!

D Make it personal Complete the sentences so they're true for you.

1 The happier I am, _____ .
2 Having money is nowhere near as important as _____ .
3 I'm really looking forward to _____ .

10.3 How easy is it to make friends where you live?

A Read the text and check (✓) the reasons the writer gives for people not being very talkative.
1. ☐ They just like being quiet.
2. ☐ They lack social skills.
3. ☐ They prefer spending time with fewer people.
4. ☐ Relaxing makes them happy.
5. ☐ They're arrogant.

Why won't they talk to me?

It's a common misconception that being a quiet person is tantamount to being a shy person. The less you speak to others, the less confident you are. While it's true that shy people may be less talkative than most, it's ¹___il_logic_al___ to assume that all quiet people are shy. For some people, being quiet is just much more pleasant than talking a lot.

A frequently made assumption is that quiet people want to talk, but can't. A more sociable person might have an ²___resist___ urge to try to make them talk more by introducing them into a group conversation. But this often ends up being ³___product___, as it just puts them in the spotlight. They might beat around the bush, fumble their words, and sound awkward, which only serves to exacerbate the problem.

On the other hand, people often think that quiet people want to be left alone. But again, this is an ⁴___rely___ assumption. Just because someone doesn't talk much in a group doesn't mean he or she doesn't want to be around other people. Quiet people might just value quality over quantity when it comes to the number of friends they have. They prefer spending time with one or two close friends, and the feeling of ⁵___depend___ that that brings, rather than hanging out in large groups. If you have a quiet friend, you're lucky – it means he or she values you.

Another ⁶___understand___ that people have about quiet people is that they're unhappy or depressed. But think about the last time you had a really long, stressful day at work, or a party you've hosted where those last guests just seem to linger on. You just wanted to be alone and have some quiet time, right? Some people are just a little happier than others during down time.

So, if you know people who don't talk much, and you're worried about any of these things, get to know them on their terms. They might be shy and want help, but they might just be naturally quiet and perfectly happy. Either way, trying to force them out of their shell is ⁷___accept___.

B Re-read and answer the questions. Is your experience with quiet people similar?

According to the writer ...
1. does encouraging quiet people to talk in groups make it easier or more difficult for them?
2. what's most important to quiet people when it comes to having friends?
3. in what situations do we all want to be alone?
4. what should we do if we're worried about quiet people?

C Complete **highlighted** words 1–7 in the text using a prefix from box A and a suffix from box B. Make any necessary spelling changes.

A
| counter ~~it~~ inter ir mis un (x2) |

B
| able (x2) ~~at~~ ence ible ing ive |

50

Have you ever met someone new by chance? 10.4

A 🔊 40 Rewrite the underlined expressions using inversions and the word in parentheses. Listen to check.

Do you believe in fate?

Aaron

Absolutely. I've just had too many strange "coincidences" happen to me not to believe in fate. Like the time I got hit by a car, and then got up and walked away. ¹If I'd crossed the street (had) _____ a second sooner or later, I would have lost my life. Then there was the time I woke up late, despite being certain I'd set my alarm as usual. I rushed out the door, but it was too late. I'd missed my bus. ²If I had to have caught it (were) _____ , I wouldn't have ended up leaving my wallet in the taxi I ended up taking to work. Luckily, the next customer in the taxi found it and returned it to me at home. ³If she hadn't returned it (had) _____ , we wouldn't have met – and ended up getting married!

Fate? What a ridiculous notion! There's absolutely no evidence for it. People have coincidences, or bad luck that turns out well in the end, and they think there's some sort of destiny guiding them through life. Well, I'm sorry, but ⁴if we believed everything (were) _____ is planned out for us, then there would be no point in carrying on with life, if you ask me. I mean, what's the point in working hard, trying to make a difference, if our future is already mapped out for us? ⁵If you wish to believe (should) _____ in fate, do so by all means. But it's not for me.

Jaden

B Circle the correct options.

1. **A:** Thanks for all your help. It's been really useful.
   B: Not at all. Should you *have / had* any more questions, just give me a call.
2. **A:** Have you heard back from Lucy yet?
   B: No, it's been a week. *If she / Had she* enjoyed our date, she would have called me by now.
3. **A:** Are you and Hilary still not speaking?
   B: No, and I'm not planning on it, either. Were she *to apologize / apologized*, I might change my mind, though.
4. **A:** I can't believe I missed you at the party last night!
   B: I know! Were I to *stayed / have stayed* just five minutes longer, I would have seen you.
5. **A:** So you're saying you're actually pleased your car broke down?
   B: Yes! *Had I not / Hadn't I* taken the train to work instead, I wouldn't have met Fiona.

C Correct the mistake in these sentences. One sentence is correct.

1. At the start of every first date, the odds are not with you. _____
2. What are the odds that we would meet like this? _____
3. The odds of see her when I was in Mexico were like a million to 1! _____
4. The lottery's a waste of time. The odds are a billion of one you'll win. _____
5. What are the odds of turning up like this? _____

D Make it personal Complete the sentences so they're true for you.

1. Had I not come to class today, _____ .
2. Were I to have met my best friend ten years ago, _____ .
3. Had I stayed at home last weekend, _____ .

51

10.5 How persuasive are you?

A Read and complete the persuasive essay with topic sentences 1–5. There's one extra sentence.

1. Where you position yourself when talking to someone is important, too.
2. As we all know, eye contact is important.
3. Communication is about so much more than words.
4. What you do with your hands says a lot about how you're feeling.
5. Copying what the other person does is another useful technique.

Using body language to get what you want

A ___ Your body language expresses a lot about what you are thinking, and this happens whether you like it or not. A lot of research has been done that proves how we compose ourselves has an effect on what we can convey, and there are several ways we can use this to our advantage.

B ___ Looking at someone directly can convey confidence and make people trust you. ¹*However / Moreover*, too much of this can intimidate the other person, and make him or her feel ill at ease. ²*However / Moreover*, it's not just about looking at someone. We can guide people to look at what we want them to look at by doing it ourselves. It's an old trick waiters use when they're showing you a menu – they look at the menu, not at you. Try it yourself some time.

C ___ Standing too close to someone can make the person uncomfortable. ³*Finally / After all*, you don't want to infringe on his or her personal space. But standing directly in front of someone can have the same effect. People are more likely to want to continue speaking to you if you stand at an angle to them. ⁴*At this point / As we all know*, they'll feel comfortable in your company and want to listen to you.

D ___ Also known as "mirroring." If you want to get people's attention, take a moment first to study their gestures. ⁵*Therefore / Next*, mimic what they do with their hands or how they're sitting. ⁶*Undoubtedly / As a result*, you don't want it to look like you're mocking them, and it's hard to get the balance just right. ⁷*Nevertheless / Next*, on a subconscious level, you'll make them feel like you're someone they can trust. ⁸*However / As a result*, they're more likely to take you seriously.

By now, you should have a range of techniques that you can use when in meetings, job interviews, and other important situations. Try some of them yourself in a more informal setting before putting them to the test in important ones.

B Re-read the essay and circle the correct options.

C Complete the sentences with these words.

| as we all know | finally | however | next | therefore |

1. Time is money. _____, you shouldn't make people wait longer than you have to.
2. _____, we're more likely to listen to people we trust.
3. First, greet people with a firm handshake. _____, offer them a seat. _____, you can get down to business.
4. Speak loudly enough for everyone to hear you. _____, don't shout!

D Look back at lessons 10.1–10.5 in the Student's Book. Find the connection between the song lines and the content of each lesson.

E ▶ 41 Listen to the five question titles from the unit, and record your answers to them. If possible, compare recordings with a classmate.

1 » 11.1 What was the last risk you took?

A ▶42 Listen to Aiden and Lily discussing the itinerary for an adventure trip in Costa Rica. Write the number of each day (1, 2, or 3) for each photo. There's one extra photo.

B ▶42 Listen again. True (T) or false (F)?
1 Lily doesn't think they should decide what to do on the first day until they arrive.
2 Aidan isn't going to go rafting.
3 During the rafting, they'll stop and walk through the jungle.
4 Lily thinks swimming with sharks is dangerous.
5 Aidan thinks the sharks might attack them.

C Correct the mistake in the extracts. Is each phrase used for hesitation (H) or encouragement (E)?
1 I'm not sure I get what it takes to jump straight into it like that. _____
2 I mean what's the worse that could happen? _____
3 These are man-eating fish. There's too much at stakes! _____
4 I mean, really, what have you gotten to lose? _____
5 I need to sleep in it before deciding. _____
6 Why not just go with a flow? _____

D Complete the conversations with one word in each blank.
1 **A:** What time does the film start?
   B: Eight, so we'd better leave at seven to be on the safe _____.
2 **A:** Have you decided what you're going to do with your inheritance?
   B: Yes, I'm going to err on the side of _____ and keep it in my savings account for now.
3 **A:** Did you hear about Ben? He's doing a parachute jump!
   A: Really? He usually _____ it safe – doesn't sound like him at all.
4 **A:** Are you going to take the part in the play?
   B: Yes, but I'm keeping my day job, so I have a safety _____ to fall back on.
5 **A:** I want to do a bungee jump, but I'm worried it's not safe.
   B: Oh, don't worry. The people who run it are trained well. It's a safe _____ nothing bad will happen.

11.2 Do you enjoy riding a bike?

A Circle the correct option to complete the conversations.

1 A: You *might as well call / could have called* us. We were worried sick about you.
   B: I'm sorry, my phone died.
2 A: Where's Sally?
   B: I'm not sure. She *might / should* be here by now. She left an hour ago.
3 A: Oh, look at those dark clouds.
   B: I know. You *might / could* want to take your umbrella if you're going out.
4 A: What's the best way to get there?
   B: Take the bus. You *shouldn't / might* have to wait too long for one at that time.
5 A: Is there a lot of room in the back of the car?
   B: Yes, lots. We *might / should* as well take the bikes with us.
6 A: Which way should I go, do you think?
   B: Take the 105. There *could / shouldn't* be too much traffic at this time of day.

B Rephrase the underlined phrases in 1–6 using modals.

1 <u>I don't expect it will be difficult to get</u> there using public transportation.   *It shouldn't be difficult*
2 <u>We're annoyed that you didn't tell us</u> we didn't need to get here so early! _____
3 What can we do about Neil? <u>He refuses to get in</u> the car. _____
4 If there are four of us, <u>it would be a good idea to get</u> a taxi. It won't cost much. _____
5 <u>It's important to wear</u> a helmet when you're biking in the city. _____
6 <u>I expected Kate to have arrived</u> by now. _____

C Complete the text with the missing modals. There may be more than one answer.

If you're someone who generally ¹_____ leave the city on weekends, but, nevertheless, wants to get out and explore, you ²_____ want to try San Francisco Urban Trail Tours. We organize weekly mountain biking tours through the wonderful nature our city has to offer. San Francisco is one of the few cities where you experience the thrill of the trail without having to leave the city. With three levels – beginner, intermediate, and advanced, it ³_____ be difficult to enjoy yourself, whatever your level. You ⁴_____ want to bring your friends, too. So what are you waiting for? You ⁵_____ as well lace up and join us this weekend! Your only regret will be that you ⁶_____ have done this much earlier!

D Make it personal Complete the sentences so they're true for you.

1 It shouldn't be too difficult to _____.
2 My parents won't _____.
3 This weekend, I might as well _____.

Are you in favor of online dating? 11.3

A Read the article and match the headings to paragraphs 1–4. There's one extra heading.
- a Being smart with your smart phone
- b Training to make an impact
- c Love (10,000 feet) in the air
- d All aboard!
- e Virtually yours

Innovative dating for today

Move over traditional dating. There are some new kids in town. It's estimated that more than 50% of Americans over 16 are single, and with more eligible adults than ever before, a number of novel new ways of finding your would-be partner are available. Here are what we think are some of the most interesting ones.

1

This is similar to traditional speed-dating in that you have three minutes to speak to someone, screening a number of people throughout the evening. However, a "coach" is present, who feeds you a series of questions while you chat, so you don't need to strike up your own conversation and can avoid any awkward silences while you fumble for words. The questions themselves get increasingly personal (e.g. When was the last time you cried?), coaxing genuine and meaningful conversation from you that aims to go beyond just "small talk."

2

Although traditional cruises have been around for a long time, singles cruises are specifically aimed at solo travelers who are looking for love or just to make new friends. They include games, speed-dating, and parties, and are generally popular with the 30–50 age range. The only problem with these is once you're on the ship, you're there for the duration. So if you don't like who you meet, you can't just leave. But at least you'll be on a cruise!

3

The problem with online dating is the anonymity can attract unpleasant, menacing people, as well as genuine singles. You end up rolling the dice without much certainty a lot of the time. A new breed of apps, however, puts the woman in control. Once you match with someone, the woman has 24 hours to make contact or the connection is lost. If you change your mind, it's easy to bail. Another one asks users to answer a daily question. The woman can then choose whether to show her photo depending on the answers she reads.

4

Though not yet a possibility, VR (Virtual Reality) dating is expected in the near future, as Internet speeds increase. This will allow you to go on a virtual reality date with someone, without having to leave the comfort of your abode. This will be a much safer way of getting to know each other before meeting for real.

B Circle the correct option to complete the sentences about the article.
1. *Over / Under* half of American adults are single.
2. Power dating, with a coach's support, requires you to be more *formal / intimate* than traditional speed dating.
3. It's *easy / difficult* to leave a singles cruise if you don't like it.
4. The new dating apps mean *more / fewer* strange people can make contact with you.
5. VR dating allows you to go on a date while you're at *home / a restaurant*.

C Match the highlighted words/phrases in the article to these meanings.
1. frightening, intimidating _____
2. start _____
3. available _____
4. evaluating to assess suitability _____
5. potential _____
6. home _____
7. escape _____
8. persuading _____
9. selecting something randomly _____

55

11.4 What does the sea make you think of?

A Complete the blanks with *a(n)*, *the*, or – (no article) and circle the correct options.

Five myths about "dangerous" animals you probably believe

ONE
1_____ bees can attack you unprovoked.

2_____ general rule is that if you leave bees alone, they'll return the favor. The same isn't true for wasps, however. Depending on how close you are to their nest or the time of year, they might sting you for seemingly no reason.

TWO
Sharks are man-eaters.

3_____ shark attacks are very, very rare. In fact, 4_____ sad statistic is that for every human killed by sharks, around two million sharks are killed by 5_____ humans.

THREE
There are lots of dangerous ⁶*animal / animals* in Australia.

While 7_____ wildlife of Australia is rich and varied, only around three people die every year of wild animal related incidents, and most of ⁸*it / them* were caused by stupidity. In comparison, around 58 ⁹*of people / people* die in Australia every year from falling out of bed!

FOUR
Wolves are dangerous to people.

Wolves are generally afraid of people. In North America in the last 100 years, 10_____ record number of people have died from wolf attacks – two.

FIVE
Run in a zig-zag to escape from 11_____ alligator.

Alligators generally avoid chasing people as they're too big to be appropriate food. But if one does chase you, run in a straight line and very fast – in 12_____ opposite direction, of course!

B Correct the mistake in these sentences. Two sentences are correct.
1 I had terrible flight a few years ago, and now I'm afraid of flying.
2 I worry about diseases a lot now that I'm getting older.
3 I've had a lot of advice about how to stay safe when traveling, but most of them wasn't very useful.
4 There has been record number of burglaries in my area recently, and that really worries me.
5 I know it sounds silly, but I'm afraid of the dark!

C ▶43 Complete the conversations with one word in each blank. Listen to check.
1 **A:** I'm reading _____ interesting article about fear and the human brain at the moment.
  B: Is that _____ article that was in *Scientist* magazine? I think I saw that.
2 **A:** Why do you think _____ rich tend to live longer?
  B: Better access to healthcare, I'd say. Most of _____ have good medical plans.
3 **A:** Are you enjoying your new job as _____ engineer?
  B: It's interesting work, though some of _____ can be quite dangerous.
4 **A:** We can take a short cut through _____ forest.
  B: No, it's too dark. That's not _____ risk I want to take.

D **Make it personal** Complete the sentences so they're true for you.
1 I'm sometimes afraid of _____.
2 The rich in my country should do more to _____.

Have you ever had an allergic reaction? 11.5

A Read the statistical report and answer the questions.

1 At what age are adults particularly at risk of accidents? _____
2 Where do falls usually occur? _____
3 For how long is a hot drink potentially dangerous to children? _____
4 What else can cause burns to children? _____
5 In which part of the house do the fewest accidents occur? _____

▲ ▲ ▲ ▲ ▲ ▲ ▲ ACCIDENTS IN THE HOME ▲ ▲ ▲ ▲ ▲ ▲ ▲

The number of injuries that ¹*occur / occurs* at home is higher than for any other location. Every year, approximately 20,000 people die because of accidents at home. More than four million children under the age of 15 experience accidents in and around the home every year and need to be taken to emergency rooms. One out of every five homes ²*report / reports* an accident each month.

Children under 5 and adults over 65 (most of these ³*is / are* over 75) are those who are most at risk. Most of the accidents with children ⁴*involve / involves* boys, while most of the accidents with adults ⁵*happen / happens* to women.

By room, the number of accidents in the home break down as follows:

LOCATIONS OF ACCIDENTS IN THE HOME	
Room/Area	Percent
Lounge	25
Kitchen	15
Bedroom	5
Bathroom	10
Stairs	35

The most common accidents involve falls. Half of these ⁶*is / are* on the stairs and the other half ⁷*is / are* from windows. Falls can be very serious and require medical attention. Unfortunately, some of the adults who fall ⁸*live / lives* alone, and may not be able to call for help immediately, especially if they lose consciousness.

A number of accidents with children ⁹*is / are* from burns or scalds, and some of these ¹⁰*include / includes* burns from hot drinks. A hot drink can scald a child for up to 15 minutes afterwards. Some of the burns also come from faulty electrical equipment, especially heaters.

There are a number of steps you can take to improve safety in and around the home, for example:

- Don't put heavy objects in high places.
- Keep windows closed when children are unattended.
- Use stair "gates" with small children.
- Use a cordless kettle so children can't pull the cord.
- Have all heaters checked for safety once a year.

For more advice and information, visit **www.saferhomes.id**

B Re-read the report and circle the correct options.

C Complete the conversations with these words. There's one extra.

| cramps | doom | hives | swelling | wheezing |

1 **A:** What's that rash on your arm?
   B: It's _____. I often get them when it's cold like this.
2 **A:** Keep applying this cream, and the _____ should go down in a day or two.
   B: Thanks, doctor.
3 **A:** I've got an impending sense of _____ about the exam.
   B: Me too, I don't think I've studied enough.
4 **A:** Are you OK?
   B: Not really, I've got stomach _____. I think that fish I ate was bad.

D Look back at lessons 11.1–11.5 in the Student's Book. Find the connection between the song lines and the content of each lesson.

E ▶44 Listen to the five question titles from the unit, and record your answers to them. If possible, compare recordings with a classmate.

57

12 » 12.1 What brands are the wave of the future?

A ▶45 Listen to a webinar on successful brand building. Number steps a–f in the order they are discussed. There's one extra step.

a ☐ Stand out from the crowd.
b ☐ Stay true to your brand.
c ☐ Reward your customers.
d ☐ Create your mission statement.
e ☐ Do your market research.
f ☐ Create a logo.

B ▶45 Listen again and choose the correct answer (a, b, or c).

1 Brands that do well sell to …
  a particular sectors of society.
  b as broad a market as possible.
  c both adults and children.
2 Building a brand your customers can identify with is important …
  a for short-term success.
  b for long-term success.
  c for both short and long-term success.
3 A mission statement is _____ a logo.
  a the same as
  b shorter than
  c different from
4 You need to study the competition so that you can …
  a sell more cheaply than other companies.
  b provide what's lacking.
  c copy their best practices.
5 A logo should …
  a help people identify you easily.
  b be simple.
  c be funny.
6 Your long-term practices should …
  a change regularly.
  b reflect your mission statement.
  c try to appeal to everyone.

C Complete the extracts from the podcast with one word in each blank.

1 All successful brand building _____ from detailed studies on the characteristics and typical behavior of the target market.
2 If you get this right, it will not only get you noticed at the beginning, but will also _____ the way for future brand loyalty.
3 While this statement might be _____ related to your slogan, it's not the same thing.
4 Maintaining your core values in practice will give _____ to strong brand loyalty, which is vital for long-term success.

D Look at the table. Then circle the correct options in 1–5.

Year	Sales of 3D TVs (millions)
2012	0.5
2013	15
2014	25
2015	12.9
2016	9.7
2017	9.6

1 After a bumpy start, sales of 3D TVs *skyrocketed / plummeted* in 2013.
2 In 2014, they continued to *level off / soar* to 25 million.
3 In 2015, sales *rose / plunged* to 12.9 million.
4 They continued to *fall / soar* in 2016 to 9.7 million.
5 Since then, they have *leveled off / risen* to about this same number..

What songs have changed the world? 12.2

A Complete 1–5 with the verbs in parentheses. Use passive forms with a gerund or an infinitive. Any surprises?

Sometimes songs don't mean what you think they do

It's often easy to interpret song lyrics how we want to, and some would argue that's the real beauty of music – that it can mean different things to different people. But sometimes we get it totally wrong.

Take U2's critically acclaimed One. ¹_____ (interpret) as a love song leads to it often being played at weddings. It would seem lead singer Bono objects to it ²_____ (use) this way, however. When he heard from fans about it, he replied, "Are you mad? It's about splitting up!"

While not a misinterpretation as such, 2012 K-Pop classic Gangnam Style has a deeper meaning than most expect. With its catchy dance track and signature move, it's easy ³_____ (see) as a lighthearted, funny song. However, it should ⁴_____ (not consider) this way, as it's actually a satire on South Korean society and those who enjoy ⁵_____ (see) as wealthy, despite not having much money and having fallen into debt.

B Use the prompts to complete the sentences.

1 We just released our new single, and we're [look forward / to / it / play] _____ on the radio.
2 We expected our first album [play] _____ everywhere, but it didn't do very well in the end.
3 [offer] _____ a recording contract was the highlight of our career.
4 The song's explicit lyrics meant it [could / not / play] _____ on the radio.
5 After our "joke" song *Hilda's Eggs*, we found it [difficult / take] _____ seriously as a band again.
6 This song is about the fact that we [couldn't stand / reject] _____ so often by record producers.

C Complete the crossword with the missing phrasal verbs in the clues. Refer to Student's Book page 128.

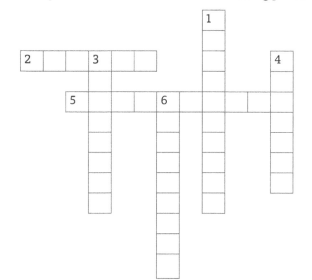

ACROSS
2 I didn't enjoy the book at first, but it slowly began to _____ _____ me.
5 It was an important song which helped raise awareness and _____ _____ real change for the better.

DOWN
1 As some artists get older, they _____ _____ their earlier success rather than trying something completely new.
3 The audience wasn't very enthusiastic at first, but after the second song, they started to _____ _____ the band.
4 It wasn't until their third album that the band's music began to _____ _____.
6 The message that the story tries to _____ _____ is one of hope in difficult circumstances.

D **Make it personal** Complete the sentences so they're true for you.

1 I would enjoy being thought of as _____.
2 When I die, I hope to be remembered for _____.
3 I really object to _____.

12.3 What futuristic programs have you seen?

A Read the article and check (✓) the statement which best reflects the writer's opinion.
1. ☐ Change is good, but not if it happens too quickly.
2. ☐ We should avoid change unless it's only for the greater good.
3. ☐ There are both positive and negative effects of change.

The future's bright – or is it?

1. It's an undisputed fact that the world is changing and will continue to do so at an unprecedented rate. Every day we make giant leaps in key areas, namely science, technology, and medicine. For the most part these changes are positive, exciting, and aimed at the greater good. But more prescient futurologists are drawing attention to the downsides, too.

2. Take driverless cars, for example. Once considered to be a wacky idea, they're now already becoming a reality. They're generally thought to be much safer as they eliminate the pitfalls of human error caused by distraction and fatigue. Cars will be able to make calculated decisions on speed instead of responding to random human reactions. But they also raise important moral questions. Let's say your driverless car is forced to swerve from a hazard in order to save you. Would it still do so if it meant hitting a pedestrian? Will its primary function be to save the driver or the public?

3. Another growing trend is that of fitness trackers, which monitor your exercise and sleep patterns. A recent case in the U.S. showed that the data collected can be used as evidence in court. A woman called 911 and claimed an intruder broke into her house while she was asleep, when, in fact, the tracker showed she was up and walking about normally. There are even apps that work with trackers specifically aimed at providing you with an alibi. But what kind of people want to provide alibis? Also, what's to stop someone from framing you for a crime by stealing your tracker?

4. Virtual Reality (VR) is another technology which is undergoing serious development at the moment. It has lots of useful applications such as gaming, training surgeons, and even dating. However, many farsighted people argue that there needs to be a lot more research done into the effects on the human brain. We already know that it gets your eyes to work in different ways from what is normal and alters your perception of distance. It's therefore dangerous to drive immediately after using a VR headset.

5. We should definitely encourage change and development, but it's worth remembering that with great change comes great opportunity, but only if it's managed appropriately and studied properly.

B Re-read the article. True (T) or false (F)?
1. The rate of change is getting slower.
2. People once thought driverless cars weren't a serious idea.
3. The example given shows that driverless cars are more dangerous for everyone.
4. The woman who called 911 was sleeping when the crime occurred.
5. The writer suggests that fitness trackers could be used in crimes.
6. The writer thinks VR headsets provide harmless entertainment.

C Find words in the article to match these definitions.
1. advances, developments made quickly (par.1) _____ (n)
2. specifically (par.1) _____ (adv)
3. having knowledge of events before they take place (par.1) _____ (adj)
4. silly, crazy (par.2) _____ (adj)
5. hidden or unseen dangers (par.2) _____ (n)
6. done without planning (par.2) _____ (adj)
7. experiencing (par.4) _____ (v)
8. having awareness of future possibilities (par.4) _____ (adj)

How unpredictable has your life been? 12.4

A ▶46 Complete the conversation using the prompts in parentheses. Listen to check.

PENNY: Hey Mike, I heard you ¹_____ (get / promote) to store manager recently.
MIKE: Yes! It was a real surprise, I can tell you.
PENNY: Oh yeah? Why's that?
MIKE: Honestly, a few weeks ago I thought I was going to ²_____ (get / fire)! I ³_____ (have / some work / do) on my apartment at the time and having to sleep on the sofa. I kept waking up late and then showing up late for work. My boss wasn't happy and I kept ⁴_____ (get / hassle) about it. And I ⁵_____ (have / my work / criticize), too, by him, because he was in a bad mood, which made me feel really pressured.
PENNY: Oh, I never realized. So what changed?
MIKE: Well, one night the store ⁶_____ (be / break into). We were looking through the CCTV and I recognized the people on the video. So I ⁷_____ (get / the police / involve) and told them everything I knew about them.
PENNY: Really? And they were arrested?
MIKE: Exactly. And my boss ⁸_____ (have / all the stolen items / recover). Anyway, needless to say, I was back in good standing, and when the manager's position became available, he gave it to me!
PENNY: Congratulations!

B Correct the mistake in these sentences. One sentence is correct.
1 Be careful crossing the road. You could have hurt if you don't look both ways. _____
2 If you don't keep up repayments, you could have repossessed your house. _____
3 I just had my manuscript accepted by the publisher! I'd almost given up hope. _____
4 After catching the thieves, Gary had his photo took with the store owner. _____
5 Don't do that here. Do you want to get arrested us? _____
6 Joanna was been pressured constantly by her boss before she suddenly announced she was leaving. _____

C Match 1–5 to endings a–e to form sentences.

1 I'm not going to drive all the way there for a 30-minute meeting. It's just not
2 Studying coding at school is really
3 I didn't think it would be worth
4 Is it worth my
5 Is it worth the

a ☐ entering the competition, but I ended up winning first prize!
b ☐ effort of calling the police? I don't think there's anything they can do.
c ☐ worth it.
d ☐ time watching this movie? I've heard it's good, but it's three hours long!
e ☐ worthwhile for kids today, given the uncertain job market in the future.

D **Make it personal** Complete the sentences so they're true for you.
1 The last time I had my photo taken _____.
2 I hate being pressured to _____.
3 I try to avoid getting hurt by _____.

12.5 What will make a better society?

A Rewrite a–e using a noun phrase.

a the number of people who work outside the home has declined steadily
there has been a steady decline in the number of people who work outside the home

b the number of people using social media has increased hugely

c criticisms of its effect on our well being have risen steadily

d the number of "clickbait" articles has increased dramatically

e the number of work opportunities has risen steeply

B Read and complete the opinion essay with your sentences from **A**.

Does social media make us happier?

1 Love it or loathe it: ¹☐ in recent times. With the increased use ²☐. Does it make us happier or sadder? Many say we now have shorter attention spans; we're more likely to be jealous of others; and we end up making unreasonable comparisons between ourselves and those we see online. I would argue, however, that the benefits far outweigh these criticisms.

2 In recent years ³☐, especially in office jobs. Many people are choosing to work from home. Access to social media makes people feel less isolated and allows them to stay connected with the outside world. It's also a way of making new connections. As someone who works from home myself, I have noticed ⁴☐, which came about through connections made on social media. This is work I wouldn't have gotten in a 9–5 office job.

3 I also believe that it has forced us to become better at critical thinking – ⁵☐. These articles use sensationalist titles and often contain spurious, unchecked facts. This might seem like a bad thing at first, but as more and more hoaxes and false news stories are exposed, people become more aware and more likely to fact-check them before sharing.

4 In conclusion, whether it really makes us happier or not, it's incredibly popular and unlikely to go away any time soon. While many fears about social media are real, I genuinely believe that overall it's a positive force.

C Re-read the opinion essay and answer the questions. Do you agree with the author?

1 What three negative effects of social media are given in the introduction (paragraph 1)?

2 What two benefits of social media are given in paragraph 2?

3 What negative aspects of "clickbait" articles are described?

D Look back at lessons 12.1–12.5 in the Student's Book. Find the connection between the song lines and the content of each lesson.

E ▶ 47 Listen to the five question titles from the unit, and record your answers to them. If possible, compare recordings with a classmate.

Selected audio scripts

1 page 3 exercises A and B
J = Janet, C = Chris

J: So Chris, is it true that your nephew Simon is starting college next month?
C: Yes! Amazing, isn't it? I still think of him as being a child, but he was eighteen this year.
J: Tell me about it. I remember his first day at school. I can still see it as if it were yesterday.
C: That reminds me. Did I ever tell you about my first day at college?
J: No?
C: Oh, it was a complete nightmare!
J: Why? What happened?
C: Well, I was really, really tired. As far as I can remember, there'd been a party the night before for all the new students, and I must have gotten to bed in the early hours. Anyway, my alarm didn't go off so I woke up late and was rushing to get to the first class. I had just enough time to get a strong cup of coffee and that woke me up enough to get to class on time ... just barely.
J: That was lucky.
C: Yeah. So anyway, about halfway through the class the effects of the coffee wore off, and I have a vague recollection of the lecturer, a young woman, speaking in a really soft voice, and ... well, I must have dozed off at the back of the class.
J: Oh no! Did the lecturer see you?
C: Ha! Oh no, it was much worse than that. Suddenly, the alarm on my phone went off. I must have set it for the wrong time the night before or something, and I jumped up in my seat, and shouted ...
J: What did you say?
C: This is so embarrassing. I shouted out, "Don't make me get up yet, Mom!" – looking right at the lecturer!
J: Oh no! Why on earth did you say that?
C: I really don't know. I must have been half asleep still, or something. As you can imagine, everyone in the class started laughing.
J: What did the lecturer say?
C: Oh, nothing really, she just looked really embarrassed. I think she was more embarrassed than me, to be honest.
J: I can imagine.
C: Anyway, as soon as the class ended, I rushed off before anyone could talk to me.
J: Oh, you poor thing.
C: I know! But come to think of it, there was a happy ending. I became good friends with that lecturer, and in the end we had a laugh about it. She even jokingly called me her "little boy" in the class!
J: Well, I hope your nephew has a better first day than you.
C: Me too!

5 page 8 exercise A
C = Charlotte, G = Gavin

C: What's up, Gavin? You seem a bit down.
G: Oh, the usual. My job.
C: What? I thought you were really enjoying it there.
G: I used to, but I've been having a really tough time there lately. I must have done something to upset my boss, because he's making things really difficult for me.
C: How so?
G: Well, he's really critical of everything I do. And he keeps giving me really tight deadlines, which he knows I won't be able to meet. It feels like he just wants to make things hard for me every day.
C: That's really too bad. So, what are you going to do?
G: I have no idea. No, actually, that's not true. I've been toying with the idea of leaving, to be honest. It's just that the job pays well, and, uh, they're helping me work towards a Master's degree.
C: OK, but is that really what you want to do?
G: I thought so, but these days I'm not so sure.
C: All right, well, if you could do anything, what would you do?
G: Well, there is one thing ...

6 page 8 exercises B and C
G: Well, there is one thing...
C: What's that?
G: I know it sounds a little far-fetched, but I'm in a band with some old school friends.
C: Oh yes, *Robot Republic*! I saw you play the other week! You were great!
G: They want me to go on tour with them over the summer. But I don't know, I mean, I'd have to leave my job and my studies. And there's a lot at stake.
C: Yes, I think you're right. Being in the band is fun and everything, but what would you do after the tour? You can't just sit around and wait for something else to fall into your lap.
G: You're right, of course. That would be really reckless. It's just that with all my problems at work, succeeding there and finishing my degree – they just seem like really unattainable goals right now.
C: Have you tried talking to your boss about how you feel?
G: Do you think that's a good idea? Maybe it will just make things worse.
C: I can't see how. Maybe he's just under a lot of pressure himself. Perhaps you could take some vacation to go on the tour. Then when you come back, you'll be feeling refreshed. You'll go the extra mile and work better. You can still work toward your degree, and, hopefully you'll be feeling better about everything.
G: You really think so?
C: It can't hurt to try. I know if you put your mind to it, you can make things work.
G: I guess, you're right. Thanks so much, Charlotte. I'm feeling much better. I'm determined to try to make this work.
C: That's the spirit!

10 page 13 exercises A, B and C
V = Valeria, L = Leon, J = Julia

V: All in all, it's been a bit of a bumpy ride to be honest. I mean, for a long time when I first started, I couldn't even get a half-decent sound out of it, and felt really out of my depth. My teacher was really encouraging though, and I put a lot of effort into it, practicing every day. I gradually started to improve, until I was about intermediate level. Then when I went to college it fell by the wayside, and I just sort of stopped playing. I recently picked it up again, and although I was a bit rusty at first, soon it all came back to me. It's surprising how much you remember after you've learned it once. It's a bit like riding a bike, I guess. In the last year I've been playing more and more, and next week I have my first concert!
L: Well, about a year ago I went to the doctor for a check-up, and he told me I needed to start doing more exercise. I'd never been much of a "sports" person, and although it's a necessary evil, I'd always hated the thought of doing any exercise. So we talked about it, and he suggested that I try going for a walk every day. That seemed doable to me, so I gave it a try. It was actually surprisingly easy and in the end it opened up a whole new world. Before I knew it I was going longer distances each day and enjoying it more and more. I was hooked! Then I started jogging, and to my surprise, I just sort of picked it up naturally. Since then I've joined a club, and I've improved by leaps and bounds. Actually, I just signed up for my first half marathon in September!
J: I've always been into computers and technology, but never really known how they work. People see me as a sort of "techy" person, but I think that's debatable. I always just sort of get by when I need to and hope for the best. Well, a few months ago I decided to sign up for a free online course in coding because I thought it looked interesting, and I absolutely loved it. Most people think it's boring, but to me it's fun, fun, fun! I'm now writing my own stuff and have just produced my first app: it helps language learners record new vocabulary they see in signs in the street.

14 page 18 exercises A and B
S = Sue, J = Jaylan

J: Hey Sue, have you read this article about dreams?
S: No, what does it say?
J: Well apparently, there are several things that influence your dreams, and some are quite unexpected.

63

Selected audio scripts

S: Oh really? I always take these things with a grain of salt. It's usually some nonsense about what star sign you are or something.
J: I know what you mean, but not this one. It's based on several scientific studies so the results are generally trustworthy.
S: So, what does it say?
J: Well, for example, bad smells can make you have bad dreams, and vice-versa.
S: Hmm, that sounds plausible.
J: Yes, according to a German study, 15 volunteers were asked to sleep in a laboratory in two groups. When they entered R.E.M. sleep–
S: R.E.M. sleep?
J: "Rapid Eye Movement." It's the stage of the sleep when you dream.
S: Oh, OK.
J: So, anyway, when they entered that, one group had foul smells pumped into the room and the other had nice smells pumped into theirs. After a few minutes they woke them up and asked them to immediately describe their dreams. And what they found was that there was a direct correlation – the nicer the smell, the nicer the dream!
S: That sounds logical. I mean, there's no doubt in my mind that strong smells have a big effect on how I feel. Especially when you don't take a shower after the gym!
J: Ha, without a shadow of a doubt. Sorry!
S: So, what else does it say?
J: Well, another study showed that regular video game players are able to take control of their dreams while asleep. It's called Lucid dreaming, and it's where dreams become lifelike. You're able to "fight off" bad dreams and take control. Just like in a video game!
S: Oh I see. How very convenient for you. I bet you're going to say next that it means you need to spend more time playing video games in the evening, right?
J: Well, I wouldn't go so far as to say that, but you know, if you think it's a good idea …
S: So, does it say anything about personality types? Or if dreams are stress-related?
J: Well, there is one thing. The jury is still out on this, but some scientists have made the claim that the more creative you are, the more likely you are to remember your dreams.
S: Now you see this is what I mean about articles about dreams. I mean, how do they define "creative"?
J: Yeah, I'm with you on this. It does seem very arbitrary. In the study they classified people according to things like how often they daydream or how imaginative they are. Not very results-oriented or objective if you ask me. Although maybe there is some truth in it. If you spend a lot of time when you're awake daydreaming and think about imaginary worlds, perhaps your brain finds it easier to move between the conscious and subconscious?
S: Listen to yourself!
J: What? I mean it! Look, why don't you take a look at the article yourself? It's very reader-friendly.
S: You know, I think I will. Believe it or not, it actually sounds quite interesting.

18 page 23 exercises A and B

M = Marta, L = Liam

M: What's that you're looking at, Liam?
L: It's an online article. It's really quite funny actually.
M: Yeah? What's it about?
L: It's about epic publicity stunts which ended up going badly. Do you want to hear about some?
M: Ooh, yes, please go on.
L: So way back in 1981, American Airlines launched the "AApass". The idea was that you pay a one-time price of $250,000, and then you have unlimited first-class tickets for the rest of your life.
M: A quarter of a million dollars? That's a lot!
L: Yes, but first-class tickets are expensive too. Think how many times you could fly in a lifetime if you wanted to. And that's exactly what customers did. Things got out of hand when customers with the ticket started flying very frequently. One guy flew to London sixteen times – in a month!
M: Wow!
L: Yes, and another frequent flier built up over 50 million air miles. Quite ironic really, since American Airlines invented frequent flyer programs.
M: So what happened?
L: Well, in the end, they realized it was a major oversight not to have anticipated customer reactions and decided to call the whole thing off. They stopped offering it in 1994.
M: Back to square one for them then! What else is there?
L: Let me see… OK, this is another good one. Have you heard of LifeLock?
M: Sure, they're the identity theft protection company, right?
L: Exactly. Well back in 2007, the CEO was so confident of their security that he published his own social security number on the website.
M: You're kidding!
L: Nope! It was a high-stakes plan, and one that fell flat on its face, too. Can you guess what happened?
M: Someone stole his identity?
L: Yes, but not just once. Thirteen times! The thieves used it to get loans and buy presents. He only found out when they called him up to ask about payment of the debt.
M: Oh dear. So his plans to demonstrate how secure the company was definitely fell through.
L: Exactly. This one is quite interesting, too. It's not so much of a publicity stunt, but it's definitely a publicity disaster.
M: Tell me.
L: So in London, there's a skyscraper in the center of the city which has a unique curved design. People call it the "walkie-talkie" because that's what it looks like. It's a huge building and cost over $250 million to build.
M: OK.
L: When they were on the verge of completing it, they noticed a glitch.
M: What was that?
L: For up to two hours every day in the summer, if the sun shines directly onto part of the building, the curved glass acts like a mirror, and sends really hot air down to the street.
M: Oh no, really?
L: Yes, and I mean really hot. Temperatures of up to 91 degrees centigrade were recorded, and it actually melted parts of cars!
M: Wow!
L: One reporter at the time was also able to fry an egg in a pan on the ground, it was that hot. But the best thing was that the building got a new nickname.
M: What's that?
L: The "fryscraper"!

22 page 28 exercises A and B

K = Kristin, N = Narrator

K: Hi everyone, and welcome to my webinar on how to become a successful online content writer. As we all know, people read websites differently from traditional books and journals. In a world where there's a multitude of free online articles, being a successful content writer means creating stunning content which people will pick out to read. Choosing a great topic will only get you so far – unless the actual content is sufficiently enjoyable to read, readers won't make it past the first paragraph. Today, I'm going to show you how to write content that brings out the best of your work.
N: Styles.
K: Successful content writers are able to work out how to write in the appropriate style for the medium. "Listicles" – those articles that have titles like "10 misconceptions people have about English", for example, are often friendly and informal. Opinion pieces, on the other hand, are often persuasive and well-researched, pointing out facts that support your argument. And that brings me to my next piece of advice …
N: Research.
K: You should always keep your research mode turned on. When you're browsing the Internet for ideas or facts, keep a bank of links to use as sources. Make sure your sources are reliable by cross-checking any facts with at least two other sources, or you might even want to delete the fact. You can just cross it out and start again.
N: Your voice.
K: While it's important to understand the key features of different styles, it's also important to craft your own unique voice. Whether it's through the things you write about or the way you say them, it's important to be original. People should be able to recognize your writing before they see your name on the page. Once you've realized that, you'll never wear out your welcome.
N: Social media.
K: Finally, once you've written your unique content, you need to get it out there. Successful content writers know how to promote themselves through social media. You should have your own, professional

Selected audio scripts

account on each platform, which can be tagged onto anything you write. It will also help you build a professional network to showcase your work.

▶ **27** *page 33 exercises A and B*

P = Presenter, S = Scott, A = Adriana, D = Darrell, M = Martha

P: Good morning, and welcome to the *Voices* podcast, where we discuss the issues that affect you. In the last episode, we talked about milestones in life, and how we view the importance of different stages of life differently. Well, we decided to go out into the neighborhood and ask people what their most important milestones have been.

P: Scott

S: Oh, no doubt about it. For me it was having little Lucy, my pride and joy. Until then I'd been kind of just sailing through life, you know? I just took one job after another, not really having any hopes or ambitions. But when Lucy was born, all of a sudden the stakes were higher. Now I had to put someone else before me in every way. So I worked hard, put myself through college in the evenings and got a much better job.

P: Adriana

A: I've always worked really hard, so when I lost my job a few years' back it was a huge shock. I had a lot of time to sit and reflect, and see how far I'd gotten off track. It took me a long time to come to terms with the situation, especially when I kept getting rejected each time I applied for something new, which made it even harder. But I'm pleased to say that I'm now working again though, and I love my job!

P: Darrell

D: Last year, after forty years of service as a bank manager, I finally decided to call it a day. At first it was really hard, because all of a sudden you've got this big, work-shaped hole in your life, you know? But that didn't last long. Fortunately, I've never been one to wallow in self-pity, and I decided I had to take charge of my situation, really take the bull by the horns, you know? I started joining clubs here and there, taking up new interests, just doing all the things I'd always wanted to. Phew! Well, I don't think I've ever been busier – nor happier!

P: Martha

M: The most important thing I've ever done, without a shadow of a doubt, was living in Brazil for two years, teaching English. Boy was it a culture shock! Until that time, I'd never even left my hometown, not even once! Being in that new situation as a foreigner, it was like being a fish out of water. I had to learn a new language, assimilate into a new culture, everything. And I won't lie to you. At times it was really tough. But I made it through the hard times. In the end I really felt like I came of age during that time. It made me a more mature person, as a result, and I'm better able to appreciate other people's differences.

▶ **31** *page 38 exercises A and B*

P = Presenter, C = Cameron

P: In the studio with me today is Cameron Mathis, from the Movement Against Patronizing Advertisements, or MAPA. So, Cameron, am I right in thinking you don't like advertising in general?

C: Oh no, in fact that's a common misconception about our organization. We do understand the need for advertising in a competitive market. In fact, some of the commercials you see currently taking the Internet by storm are really rather good. On top of that, there are a multitude of services many of us use today that are free, thanks to the revenue generated by advertising.

P: So, what is it you're taking a stand against then?

C: Well, what we really take offense at is the way commercials seem to want to treat us like children.

P: How do you mean, exactly?

C: Take company mascots, for example. You've got an airline that uses a cartoon-style plane with a big, sappy face on the front, grinning inanely at us like it's right out of a children's book. I mean, aren't we intelligent enough to understand what an airplane is? Then you have the workers in a commercial for an electric company with juvenile, smiling faces and huge eyes. These images wouldn't look out of place in a children's TV show, but in commercials? To make matters worse, they speak in clichés, use childish language and speak directly to us like we're infants. And to add insult to injury, they all come together at the end to sing a catchy jingle that sounds more like a nursery rhyme.

P: But what's the problem, really? Surely they're just aiming for a broad appeal?

C: The problem, aside from the lack of respect for their consumers, is it's leading to a general dumbing-down of society. When people are bombarded with these images and sounds all day, every day, they begin to feel they're acceptable. And as if that wasn't enough, people accept some of the ridiculous claims made by these companies. You know the sort of thing I mean, "This sugary drink will make you healthier." The people behind these ads really need to take the blame for this.

P: But aren't some ads specifically aimed at children?

C: Some are, yes. But how many children do you know with a mortgage or with bills to pay?

P: I get your point. So, what does MAPA intend to do? Take legal action against companies that advertise in this way?

C: Oh, no, no, no. For a start, we're not out to make money off this. Besides, it's not a legal issue. It's a moral and cultural one. And since people create culture, it's people who need to take matters into their own hands. Don't buy products from companies that treat you like a child. Write to them or post on their social media, asking them why they view us like this. We need to take a stand against this together, and that's why we're trying to raise awareness with our own campaigns. We're not idiots, after all. And it's time they stopped treating us as if we were.

P: Cameron, thanks very much for joining us today.

C: Thank you.

▶ **34** *page 43 exercises B and C*

J = Jasmin (newsreader), H = Henry (reporter), D = Dorothy (school principal)

J: In education news, the government has announced plans to introduce regular mindfulness training in elementary schools as part of the state curriculum. It says that recent studies have shown that regular mindfulness training in schools helps children become calm, focused, and creative so that they work better both in class and at home. Over to our education correspondent, Henry Coleman, with more information on the story.

H: Thanks, Jasmin. I'm here at Grangeville Elementary, where in the last year students have been having regular mindfulness classes as part of their daily routine. And joining me is the school principal, Dorothy Quinn, to tell us more about it. Good morning, Dorothy. How did this project come about?

D: Good morning. Well, we decided to introduce the training a year ago. There was some opposition from a few parents at the time, who felt it was a waste of time in the school day, so we decided to make it optional, and about half the children took part. We felt the benefits would outweigh the time factor, and, so far at least, it would appear that we've been proved right.

H: Interesting. So, what happens in a mindfulness class?

D: We usually start with what we call "deep-belly breathing". The children put their hands on their stomachs and we ask them to focus on their breathing, feeling the air being drawn in. They then look at their hands, and we ask them to admire their form and what they do. Then we move on to simple stretching and walk slowly around the room, while they continue to focus on their breathing.

H: It looks as if it's quite simple.

D: It does, but believe me, it takes a lot of concentration.

H: So, what benefits have you found from the training?

D: Well, for starters, the children in the program consistently outperform those who opted out, both on tests and in day-to-day schoolwork.

H: Really?

D: Yes. In fact, as the program continued and parents started seeing a difference, more and more children joined the program, and they now outnumber considerably those who didn't take part. We're also finding that their concentration levels outlast the others, too. They're able to focus for much longer in class. We've also been using the training to replace some traditional discipline punishments, too.

H: In what way?

65

Selected audio scripts

D: Well, if a child was particularly unruly in class before, or got in trouble for something, he or she might have had detention for an hour after school, doing extra work. We've replaced that with a mindfulness session, and have found that these kids outgrow their immature behavior much more quickly. Rather than trying to outsmart the teachers and break the rules, they're being much more cooperative.
H: This all sounds fascinating, Dorothy, thank you. I may try it myself!
D: You should!

38 page 48 exercises A and B

R = Ron, E = Eva

R: Did I ever tell you about my so-called friend James, the one I had at high school?
E: No, you didn't. Why "so-called"?
R: Well, I guess it goes without saying he was the worst friend I've ever had.
E: Why? What did he do?
R: Well, I met him during my senior year. He had just moved to the area and just started at our school. He was a breath of fresh air, really livened up the place.
E: Why do you say that?
R: Er, he was just really good fun. The life of the party, you know? We hit it off immediately. We went out at weekends and he took me to parties. Oh, what a riot he was!
E: So, why wasn't he a good friend?
R: After a while, the cracks in our friendship started to appear. Like, he kept insisting on coming over to my house rather than going out or to his. And he started being really critical of everything I did. Sometimes he'd just try to embarrass me, you know? It goes without saying that I was starting to get a bit suspicious. Anyway, one day he was over and we were playing a video game. All of a sudden he just got up and left, no words, nothing. Later that evening I realized my camera had disappeared.
E: Oh no, had he taken it?
R: I think so, though I can never be sure. I looked everywhere, and I remember I'd showed it to him the day before.
E: So, did you confront him about it?
R: Easier said than done! He stopped talking to me at school and was always surrounded by another group of friends. I know I should have said something, but, truth be told, I just felt too embarrassed, you know, and betrayed.
E: Oh, that's awful. You know I lost a good friend too, once.
R: Really? What happened?

39 page 48 exercise C

R: Really? What happened?
E: It was my best friend, Judy. We went back a long way. I mean we'd been friends since we were five. We went everywhere together, you know? Real birds of a feather.
R: Yeah, I've had a couple of friends like that.
E: Yeah, and we really understood each other, you know? Our conversations always went beneath the surface. I mean we didn't always see eye to eye, but we understood each other – sometimes without even having to speak.
R: So, what happened?
E: When we were in our early twenties, she met this guy –
R: Ah-ha!
E: No, I mean we'd both had boyfriends before, but always stayed close. But this time it was different. She would spend all her time with him. It got to the point where she stopped returning my calls. I was really upset and I really missed her.
R: Are they still together?
E: I have no idea. Last I heard he had gotten a new job in Illinois, and they moved there. I haven't heard from her since.
R: Oh, that's sad.
E: Yeah, it is. But at least we have each other now, right?
R: That goes without saying!

42 page 53 exercises A and B

A = Aiden, L = Lily

A: So, what's first on the itinerary then?
L: OK, well, we arrive in the capital, San José, at lunchtime, and then spend the day there relaxing. We can either go sightseeing or just explore the area near the hotel. Best to just see how we feel when we get there, I think. Then the next morning, first thing, we head out to the Pacuare River for white-water rafting.
A: Wow, OK ...
L: What's wrong?
A: Um ... it's just that I've never done it before, and the brochure says it's a tough river, not for beginners. I'm not sure I have what it takes to jump straight into it like that.
L: Really? We could just play it safe and go on one of the calmer rivers if you like.
A: Ah no, it's fine. Let's throw caution to the wind. It's supposed to be an adventure vacation after all, right? I mean, what's the worst that could happen?
L: That's the spirit! And it's all organized by a reputable company with trained first-aid personnel in case anything goes wrong ... so there's kind of a safety net. Also, the river goes through the jungle, and you can see all sorts of animals like toucans and howler monkeys.
A: Fantastic. So, what's next?
L: OK, so Day 3 we go to Cahuita National park, and go hiking through the jungle for a few hours in the morning and end up at the beach. In the afternoon, we need to decide what we're going to do. There's snorkeling, zip lining and even swimming with sharks!
A: Ooh, I like the sound of that.
L: Really? I think it sounds terrifying! These are man-eating fish. There's too much at stake!
A: Don't be silly, they wouldn't let you swim with them if it was dangerous in any way. It's a safe bet they won't attack you. I mean really, what have you got to lose?
L: Hmmm, not sure. I need to sleep on it before deciding.
A: Well, we don't have to decide until we're there, do we? Why not just go with the flow? We can see what other people are doing.
L: OK then, good idea. So, day 4 ...

45 page 58 exercises A and B

Hello, and welcome to the latest webinar in the *Building your Business* series. Today we're going to be looking at building a successful brand in five simple steps. This is one of the most important aspects of your new business. If you get it right, you'll see sales of your product soar. So, if you're ready, let's begin. If you have any questions, please type them in the chat box and I'll answer them at the end of the webinar.

Step 1 – All successful brand building stems from detailed studies on the characteristics and typical behavior of the target market. Almost all successful brands are aimed at specific, niche markets. Find out what your potential customers' values and desires are, and then create a brand image they can relate to. If you get this right, it will not only get you noticed at the beginning, but will also pave the way for future brand loyalty. We'll come back to this later.

Step 2 – Figure out exactly what your core values are and how to express them concisely in a mission statement. This is an important foundation for all your future work, so don't rush it. While this statement might be closely related to your slogan, it's not the same thing. For example, Nike's slogan is "Just Do It", whereas its mission statement is, "to bring inspiration and innovation to every athlete in the world."

Step 3 – Differentiate your product from other brands. You need a USP – a unique selling point – and again this means doing your research, this time on the competition. Find out what your closest competitors do well, and what they don't do so well, as this is where you can come in and fill the gap. If your brand is too similar to others in the market, you may well find that after any initial success, the novelty will wear off and sales will plummet.

Step 4 – While it may seem obvious, the next step is perhaps the most important part of brand building. It's worth spending considerable time and money on it. You want something which clearly embodies the values and mission of your business. You also want something which is attractive and easily recognizable.

Step 5 – If you've followed all the steps so far, then you've built the foundations for a successful brand. But that's only the beginning. An outsider should be able to read your mission statement, look at what you do and see a perfect match. Maintaining your core values in practice will give rise to strong brand loyalty, which is vital for long-term success. A big product launch can cause sales to skyrocket, but long-term brand loyalty is important for continued success, even if it just means that sales level off to profitable numbers. Be true to your customers, and they'll be loyal to you.

OK, so I see we have some questions coming in. Let's start with this one from ...

Answer key

Unit 1
1.1
A a 2 b 5 c 1 d 4 e 3
B 1 T 2 F 3 F 4 T 5 F
C 1 wore off 2 took off 3 pull off
   4 doze off 5 ring 5 rushed off
D Students' own answers

1.2
A 1 is 2 taste 3 has 4 seems 5 say
B 1 vary 2 fail 3 seems 4 has 5 takes
   6 helps 7 is 8 have 9 discovers
   10 make
C Possible answers: 1 isn't 2 thinks
   3 doesn't like 4 is 5 have been
D Students' own answers

1.3
A It has bad advice (for those who want to work well).
B 1 It has to be perfect. 2 Don't be rude.
   3 Always work in the same place.
   4 Keep up with the world.
   5 Question everything.
C 1 mind **wander** for a while
   2 keep tuning **out** 3 it hit **me**
   4 zero **in** on 5 pop **into** her head
   6 stay on **top** of things

1.4
A 1 have been 2 've seen 3 had made
   4 had been trying 5 have described
   6 had ever done 7 haven't watched
   8 created
B 1 has 2 had 3 has had
   4 hasn't helped 5 have come 6 had
   7 has
C 1 c 2 d 3 a 4 e 5 b

1.5
A 1 I'd just finished 2 had been snowing
   3 had just stopped 4 had driven 5 saw
   6 was 7 had been looking 8 went
   9 got 10 We've had
B 1 nothing but sheer 2 I did nothing but
   3 all but certain 4 couldn't help but
C 1 face, for 2 asking, know 3 what, give
D 1 phrasal verb with *off: shake it off*
   2 the grammar: subject-verb agreement (collective nouns)
   3 creativity
   4 the grammar: using perfect tenses
   5 a dream that came true
E Students' own answers

Unit 2
2.1
A 1 no 2 He's critical. 3 leaving his job
   4 no
B To go on tour with his band. Yes, she encourages him to do it.
C 1 far-fetched 2 fall, lap 3 unattainable goals 4 extra mile 5 work toward
   6 put, mind

D 1 Go the extra mile
   2 Never try to meet people's expectations
   3 If you put your mind to it
   4 don't wait for them to fall into your lap
E 1 c 2 e 3 b 4 a

2.2
A 1 have 2 to 3 don't 4 isn't 5 hasn't
B 1 too, are, didn't, They're 2 might, have
   3 take 4 to, haven't, didn't
C 1 doesn't 2 have 3 does 4 either
   5 might
D Students' own answers

2.3
A 1 B 2 D 3 A 4 C
B 1 Ella 2 the extra statement 3 Jerome
   4 Alison 5 Brynn
C 1 crave, peace and quiet 2 convey, sense of 3 cater, tastes 4 upscale, restaurants

2.4
A 1 so 2 such 3 so, such 4 so 5 so
   6 so
B 1 b 2 c 3 c 4 a 5 b 6 a
C 1 ~~so much~~ so many 2 ~~such big~~ such a big
   3 ~~so~~ so much 4 ~~such~~ so much
D 1 drowsy 2 boost 3 dragging 4 hectic
   5 sleep
E Students' own answers

2.5
A He likes them both.
B 1 each has its pros and cons 2 In addition
   3 However 4 on the other hand
   5 Although 6 the two areas are both
C 1 has its pros and cons
   2 In addition, it has a swimming pool.
   3 Our dining room, on the other hand / On the other hand, our dining room
   4 are both cheap places to live.
D 1 being guided to a goal 2 the importance of home 3 being alone 4 the grammar: using *so many* and *so much* 5 comparing apartments
E Students' own answers

Unit 3
3.1
A Valeria: 3 Leon: 6 Julia: 5
B 1 Julia 2 Valeria 3 Leon 4 Julia
   5 Valeria 6 Leon
C 1 depth 2 effort 3 rusty 4 picked
   5 leaps 6 debatable 7 get
D Students' own answers

3.2
A Students' own answers
B 1 What this means is to
   2 we think relates back to
   3 Why this became so popular
   4 What's interesting is that
   5 Where it came from was

   6 What it would do was
   7 What we know about this expression is
   8 we don't really know
C 1 d, S 2 e, O 3 a, O 4 b, S 5 c, S
D 1 extent 2 least 3 will 4 respects
E Students' own answers

3.3
A 1 The Motivator 2 The Entertainer
   3 The Storyteller 4 The Animator
   5 The Lecturer
B 1 F 2 NI 3 NI 4 T 5 T
C 1 spread the word 2 keep your word 3 by word of mouth 4 take back your words 5 have the final word 6 tripping over words 7 get a word in edgewise

3.4
A 1 Growing up 2 Starting 3 Encouraged
   4 Arriving 5 meeting 6 Feeling
B 1 Before becoming famous
   2 Growing up in Pennsylvania
   3 Working as a support act
   4 Hoping to become a soccer player
   5 Signing her first modeling contract
C 1 ~~learn~~ learned 2 ~~Where~~ When 3 ~~had~~ having 4 ~~hearing~~ heard 5 ~~taking~~ taken
D Students' own answers

3.5
A c
B 1 b 2 a 3 d
C 1 beginning 2 while 3 time 4 Then
   5 First 6 matter
D 1 foreign languages
   2 slang expressions
   3 words and self-expression
   4 the grammar: how parents help/influence their children
   5 accomplishing something if you try
E Students' own answers

Unit 4
4.1
A 2, 5 and 6
B 1 15 2 dream 3 control 4 fight
   5 remember 6 daydream
C 1 ~~gram~~ grain 2 ~~worry~~ doubt 3 ~~With~~ Without 4 ~~long~~ far 5 ~~judge~~ jury
D 1 b 2 e 3 a 4 f 5 c 6 d

4.2
A 1 Little did I know
   2 Never again will I be late
   3 rarely does my staff play
   4 Not since my previous job had I worked
   5 did I understand
B 1 Nowhere could I find my keyboard!
   2 Only after I got home did I realize I had the wrong bag.
   3 Rarely do we play April Fool's Day pranks in my country.

67

Answer key

    4 Little did he know, we'd switched his laptop for a pizza box!
    5 Not since I was a teenager had I felt so embarrassed.
C 1 wreaking 2 breathe 3 clogged 4 flee
D Students' own answers

4.3
A 1
B 1 b 2 c 3 a 4 a 5 b
C 1 break-in 2 throwaway 3 wipeout 4 crackdown 5 cover-up 6 tip-off 7 takeover
D Students' own answers

4.4
A 1 e 2 b 3 d 4 c 5 a
B 1 in which 2 whom 3 about which 4 towards which 5 which 6 most of whom
C 1 S,S 2 S,Z 3 Z,S 4 S,Z

4.5
A 1 c 2 e 3 a 4 d 5 f 6 b
B 1 debate 2 strongly 3 irrespective 4 claims 5 argue
C 1 the truth always comes out 2 on the table 3 up to us 4 conceal information 5 banned from
D 1 dreams (vs. reality) 2 the grammar: emphatic inversion 3 illogical vs. logical thinking 4 our eyes and our emotions 5 the value of freedom (vs. incarceration)
E Students' own answers

Unit 5
5.1
A 1 T 2 F 3 T 4 F
B 1 the year the AApass was launched
    2 the cost of the AApass, in dollars
    3 the number of air miles one passenger accumulated
    4 the year they stopped selling the AApass
    5 the year the CEO of LifeLock published his social security number on the company website
    6 the number of times his identity was stolen
    7 the cost of the "walkie talkie" building in dollars
    8 the temperature recorded on the street
C 1 oversight, call 2 stakes 3 through 4 verge, glitch
D 1 pull 2 face 3 one 4 to 5 hand
E Students' own answers

5.2
A 1 Given 2 as 3 aim 4 effort 5 Thanks 6 view
B 1 c 2 b 3 e 4 a 5 d
C 1 fresh 2 get 3 through 4 anew 5 page 6 to
D Students' own answers

5.3
A 2
B 1 Vanda 2 Steve 3 extra comment 4 Steve 5 Carla
C 1 held on to 2 took stock 3 went to great lengths 4 dwell on 5 keep (things) in perspective 6 put (failures) behind you
D Students' own answers

5.4
A Possible answers: 1 me / my 2 the government's / insurance companies' 3 people / women 4 this person's / his 5 her / my date's
B 1 is 2 ~~who~~ 3 ~~they~~ them 4 ~~made~~ making / to make 5 ~~he's~~ him
C 1 with 2 out 3 on, up 4 off 5 to, up

5.5
A 1
B 1 Broadly speaking 2 Essentially 3 Clearly 4 Admittedly 5 Incidentally 6 Obviously 7 Frankly
C 1 entail 2 airtight, spells out 3 put together, turned it down, redo it
D 1 failure / letting someone down 2 New Year's Day and resolutions / the grammar: not using formal conjunctions and prepositions 3 effort and not being successful 4 relationships 5 bad drivers
E Students' own answers

Unit 6
6.1
A 1 b 2 d 3 a 4 c
B 1 a 2 c 3 c 4 b 5 a
C 1 pick out 2 brings out 3 work out 4 pointing out 5 cross (it) out 6 wear out
D Students' own answers

6.2
A 1 Unless 2 even if 3 in case 4 as long as 5 whether or not
B 1 in case 2 as long as 3 unless 4 whether or not 5 even if
C 1 the theater 2 curiosity 3 sync 4 10 5 patience 6 sheer habit
D Students' own answers

6.3
A 1 c 2 a 3 e 4 d 5 extra topic 6 b
B 1 T 2 F 3 F 4 F 5 T 6 T
C 1 sniffed 2 clasped 3 twitching 4 fluttered 5 fidgeting

6.4
A 1 do 2 does 3 am 4 do 5 didn't
B 1 did like 2 has been 3 does like 4 is open 5 did hate
C 1 colorful 2 dull 3 amazing 4 creative 5 bizarre 6 original 7 vibrant 8 unimaginative 9 inspiring
    Word: thought-provoking

6.5
A bizarre
B 1 d 2 a 3 b 4 c
C 1 b 2 c 3 d 4 a
D 1 paper books (and not electronic ones) 2 using *out of* 3 expressions with *heaven* (Roald Dahl title) 4 the grammar: using auxiliaries as rejoinders 5 dreams (and the immigrant experience)
E Students' own answers

Unit 7
7.1
A 1 b 2 a 3 b 4 c
B 1 Adriana 2 Darrell 3 Martha 4 Adriana 5 Scott 6 Martha
C 1 came of age 2 take charge of 3 gotten off track 4 the stakes were higher 5 come to terms with 6 made it through
D 1 rat 2 worms 3 cat 4 chickened 5 horse's
E Students' own answers

7.2
A 1 will have gotten 2 will have been acknowledged 3 will have had 4 will have exercised / been exercising 5 won't have been 6 will have lived
B 1 will have ~~been~~ earned 2 will have ~~been traveling~~ traveled 3 Correct 4 won't have ~~been coming~~ come 5 will have worked / will have been working 6 will have **been** allocated
C 1 will have been working 2 will have retired 3 will have been fired, will have been forced 4 will have saved 5 will have lost
D Students' own answers

7.3
A dishonest
B 1 C 2 D 3 B 4 extra sentence 5 E 6 A
C 1 facial 2 informed 3 daily 4 evolutionary 5 crucial 6 early 7 rudimentary 8 unfair 9 fair

7.4
A 1 It's not how old you are that
    2 It wasn't the first time that
    3 It's not just young people who
    4 It was 100-year-old Ida Keeling who
    5 It's not your age that
    6 It's only your belief in yourself
B 1 only respect that I feel
    2 your attitude that determines
    3 their perspective on life that
    4 a belief in themselves that
    5 their achievements that leave
C 1 act 2 pushing 3 conform 4 hand 5 wise 6 heart
D Students' own answers

7.5
A experience
B 1 response 2 suited 3 see 4 fit 5 capacity 6 consideration

C 1 receptive 2 proactive 3 attentive
  4 dynamic
D 1 possibly 2 interrupting 3 kind
  4 run 5 Would
E 1 getting married (life stages)
  2 the future and the grammar: converting future continuous to future perfect continuous 3 babies 4 human behavior
  5 jobs and making a living
F Students' own answers

Unit 8
8.1
A 1, 3, 5, 6
B 1 F 2 T 3 T 4 F 5 F 6 T
C 1 c 2 a, b 3 a 4 e 5 d
D 1 matters 2 top 3 enough 4 insult
E Students' own answers

8.2
A 1 make 2 that 3 refund 4 weren't
  5 look
B 1 you listen to your customers 2 your company give me a refund 3 you make customers aware of your policy first 4 this dress weren't so expensive 5 you be more polite when taking orders 6 you give me a bigger seat
C 1 know 2 reassess 3 write 4 wasn't
  5 be 6 give
D Students' own answers

8.3
A 1 e 2 b 3 c 4 a
B 1 worse 2 meal time 3 the flight attendant asks them not to 4 used baby products 5 acceptable
C 1 lengths 2 upon 3 saw 4 way
  5 take

8.4
A 1 For all the 2 Whatever 3 However
  4 As useful as 5 Much as
B 1 d 2 b 3 e 4 a 5 c
C Across: 1 profit 3 charge 5 borrow
  6 tax
  Down: 2 inherit 4 loan

8.5
A 3
B 1 rectify 2 avail 3 fact 4 resolve
  5 happy 6 satisfaction 7 legal 8 steps
  9 forward
C 1 avail 2 assist 3 a response
  4 Notwithstanding 5 resolve / rectify
D 1 bad customer service and advertising
  2 the grammar: *wish* + subjunctive
  3 travel and being far away
  4 making ends meet / money and the grammar: combining sentences with adverb clauses
  5 getting satisfaction by phone
E Students' own answers

Unit 9
9.1
A 1
B 1 d 2 b 3 a 4 c
C 1 b 2 c 3 a 4 a 5 b
D 1 outweigh 2 outperform 3 outnumber
  4 outlast 5 outgrow 6 outsmart
E Students' own answers

9.2
A 1 are believed to help you
  2 can be expected to make you
  3 is known to be effective
  4 are thought to be good
  5 is believed to hydrate your body
  6 is known to come from other sources
  7 was reported to make kids
B 1 are reported to be successful
  2 are thought to use
  3 is believed to be
  4 is known not to work.
C 1 coming down with 2 grew out of
  3 watching out for 4 go through with
  5 gave up on
D Students' own answers

9.3
A 2
B 1 Darren 2 Mike 3 Angela 4 Celia
C 1 F 2 F 3 T 4 F 5 T
D 1 ending 2 desire 3 belief
  4 discussion 5 choices 6 blanket
  7 mate 8 rearing

9.4
A 1 to change 2 from doing 3 make
  4 to replace 5 on keeping 6 to start
  7 not to do 8 do 9 his 10 enjoy
B 1 dissuaded me **from** eating 2 ~~stopping~~ to stop 3 you ~~to~~ join 4 ~~to eat~~ from eating
  5 Correct 6 ~~lift~~ lifting
C 1 threaten 2 weaken 3 worsen
  4 soften 5 lengthen 6 strengthen
  7 freshen
D Students' own answers

9.5
A against
B 1 Weight loss 2 Confidence
  3 Awareness 4 Education 5 provide
  6 lead 7 create 8 slow
C 1 ~~weight loss~~ lose weight
  2 ~~Provide a~~ A safe environment:
  3 ~~concentration~~ concentrate at work better.
D 1 correctly 2 mind 3 judgment
E 1 *out-* verbs 2 three word phrasal verbs (*give up on*) 3 surviving challenging situations 4 the grammar: overview of verb patterns (pattern a) 5 celebrating beauty regardless of weight, etc.
F Students' own answers

Unit 10
10.1
A 1 Ron's camera 2 He stopped talking to Ron.
B 1 Ron 2 James 3 James 4 James
  5 James 6 Ron
C 1 They'd been friends since they were five.
  2 Sometimes they understood each other without the need to speak.
  3 Judy met her boyfriend in their early twenties.
  4 Judy stopped returning her calls.
  5 Judy and her boyfriend moved to Illinois.
D 1 c 2 a 3 f 4 e 5 g 6 b 7 d
E 1 telling 2 said 3 told 4 saying
  5 Say

10.2
A 1 the harder 2 whole 3 near
  4 every bit 5 quite 6 far 7 bit
B 1 The more you exercise, the healthier you'll be.
  2 How you feel is much more important than how old you are.
  3 Eating well is just as essential as exercising / exercise (verb or noun).
  4 Having many friends is nowhere near as beneficial as having good friends.
  5 My brother and I aren't quite as close as we used to be.
  6 Making friends online is slightly easier than making friends face-to-face.
C 1 b 2 a 3 c 4 f 5 e 6 d
D Students' own answers

10.3
A Check 1, 3 and 4.
B 1 more difficult
  2 quality (over quantity)
  3 after a long day at work or a party that goes on too long
  4 get to know them on their own terms
C 1 illogical 2 irresistible
  3 counterproductive 4 unreliable
  5 interdependence 6 misunderstanding
  7 unacceptable

10.4
A 1 Had I crossed the street
  2 Were I to have caught it
  3 Had she not returned it
  4 Were we to believe everything
  5 Should you wish to believe
B 1 have 2 Had she 3 to apologize
  4 have stayed 5 Had I not
C 1 ~~not with~~ against 2 correct 3 ~~see~~ seeing 4 billion ~~of~~ **to** one 5 the odds of **[subject]** turning up
D Students' own answers

10.5
A A 3 B 2 C 1 D 5
B 1 However 2 Moreover 3 After all
  4 At this point 5 Next 6 Undoubtedly
  7 Nevertheless 8 As a result
C 1 Therefore 2 As we all know
  3 Next, Finally 4 However

Answer key

D 1 the nature of friendship 2 the life span (living forever) 3 double affixation (*un-* and *-ful*) 4 the grammar: inverted conditional sentences 5 persuading someone

E Students' own answers

Unit 11

11.1
A 1 d 2 a 3 c
B 1 T 2 F 3 F 4 T 5 F
C 1 ~~get~~ have, H 2 ~~worse~~ worst, E 3 ~~stakes~~ stake, H 4 ~~gotten~~ got, E 5 ~~in~~ on, H 6 ~~a~~ the, E
D 1 side 2 caution 3 plays 4 net 5 bet

11.2
A 1 could have called 2 should 3 might 4 shouldn't 5 might 6 shouldn't
B 1 It shouldn't be difficult to get
  2 You could have told us
  3 He won't get in
  4 we might as well get
  5 You should wear
  6 Kate should have arrived
C 1 won't 2 might 3 shouldn't 4 might 5 might 6 could
D Students' own answers

11.3
A 1 b 2 d 3 a 4 e
B 1 Over 2 intimate 3 difficult 4 fewer 5 home
C 1 menacing 2 strike up 3 eligible 4 screening 5 would-be 6 abode 7 bail 8 coaxing 9 rolling the dice

11.4
A 1 – 2 The 3 – 4 a 5 – 6 animals 7 the 8 them 9 people 10 a 11 an 12 the
B 1 **a** terrible flight 2 correct 3 most of ~~them~~ **it** 4 **a** record number 5 correct
C 1 an, the 2 the, them 3 an, it 4 the, a
D Students' own answers

11.5
A 1 over 65 2 on the stairs and out of windows 3 15 minutes 4 faulty equipment (e.g. heaters) 5 the bedroom
B 1 occur 2 reports 3 are 4 involve 5 happen 6 are 7 are 8 live 9 are 10 include
C 1 hives 2 swelling 3 doom 4 cramps
D 1 the word *safe*
  2 the grammar: special uses of modals (*won't* for refusal)
  3 dating and love
  4 the grammar: definite and indefinite articles (pattern b, lightning)
  5 safety (horseback riding)
E Students' own answers

Unit 12

12.1
A 1 e 2 d 3 a 4 f 5 b
B 1 a 2 c 3 c 4 b 5 a 6 b
C 1 stems 2 pave 3 closely 4 rise
D 1 skyrocketed 2 soar 3 plunged 4 fall 5 leveled off

12.2
A 1 Being interpreted 2 being used 3 to be seen 4 not be considered 5 being seen
B 1 looking forward to it being played 2 to be played 3 Being offered 4 couldn't be played 5 difficult to be taken 6 couldn't stand being rejected
C Across: 2 grow on 5 bring about
  Down: 1 fall back on 2 warm up to 4 catch on 6 get across
D Students' own answers

12.3
A 3
B 1 F 2 T 3 F 4 F 5 T 6 F
C 1 leaps 2 namely 3 prescient 4 wacky 5 pitfalls 6 random 7 undergoing 8 farsighted

12.4
A 1 got promoted 2 get fired 3 was having some work done 4 getting hassled 5 was having my work criticized 6 was broken into 7 got the police involved 8 had all the stolen items recovered
B 1 ~~have~~ be/get 2 have your house repossessed 3 Correct 4 ~~took~~ taken 5 get us arrested 6 ~~been~~ being
C 1 c 2 e 3 a 4 d 5 b
D Students' own answers

12.5
A a there has been a steady decline in the number of people who work outside the home
  b there has been a huge increase in the number of people using social media
  c there has been a steady rise in criticisms of its effect on our well being
  d there has been a dramatic increase in the number of "clickbait" articles
  e there has been a steep rise in the number of work opportunities
B 1 b 2 c 3 a 4 e 5 d
C 1 shorter attention spans, jealousy, and making unfair comparisons between ourselves and others.
  2 It allows us to stay connected and can provide work opportunities.
  3 sensationalist titles and unchecked "facts"
D 1 trends and the word *wave*
  2 the grammar: passive forms with gerunds and infinitives (pattern 2 in active form)
  3 the future
  4 the grammar: the passive and causative with *get* (causative passive: *get* = *have*)
  5 improving the world
E Students' own answers

58 St Aldates
Oxford
OX1 1ST
United Kingdom

ISBN: 978-84-668-2091-2
DL: M-4708-2016
First Edition: November 2016
© Richmond / Santillana Global S.L.

All rights reserved. No part of this book may be reproduced, stored in a retrieval system or transmitted in any form by any means, electronic, mechanical, photocopying, recording or otherwise, without the prior permission in writing of the Publisher.

Richmond publications may contain links to third party websites. We have no control over the content of these websites, which may change frequently, and we are not responsible for the content or the way it may be used with our materials. Teachers and students are advised to exercise discretion when assessing links.

Publishing Director: Deborah Tricker

Editors: Deborah Goldblatt, Laura Miranda, Shona Rodger

Proofreader: Cathy Heritage

Project and Cover Design: Lorna Heaslip

Layout: Dave Kuzmicki

Picture Researcher: Magdalena Mayo, Arnos Design

Illustrator: Pablo Velarde

Digital Content: Luke Baxter

Audio Recording: Motivation Sound Studios

Photos:
Kirby Lee - USA TODAY Sports; ALAMY/ Andres Rodriguez, PhotoAlto, Loop Images Ltd.; GETTY IMAGES SALES SPAIN/ Kim Kulish, Carolyn Cole, Stokbyte, Paul Drinkwater/NBCU Photo Bank, David Freund; ISTOCKPHOTO/Getty Images Sales Spain; ROALD DAHL NOMINEE LTD; SHUTTERSTOCK NETHERLANDS,B.V.; Andrew Smith; ARCHIVO SANTILLANA

The Publisher has made every effort to trace the owner of copyright material; however, the Publisher will correct any involuntary omission at the earliest opportunity.

Impressão e acabamento: Meta Brasil

Lote: 800431
Lote: 290520912